CONTINUUM

The First Songbook of

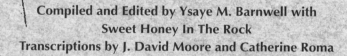

Sweet Honey In The Rock

Compiled and Edited by Ysaye M. Barnwell with
Sweet Honey In The Rock
Transcriptions by J. David Moore and Catherine Roma

PUBLISHED BY

CONTEMPORARY
A CAPPELLA
PUBLISHING

EXCLUSIVELY DISTRIBUTED BY

HAL•LEONARD®
CORPORATION

Transcriptions utilized Finale Software v.3.7.2 on a Macintosh Centris 610 computer.
The music font used is Golden Age by Donald Rice.

ISBN 0-634-01274-6

Cover design by Ann Ahearn
Cover and biography photos by Dwight Carter
Left to right: Shirley Childress Saxton, Nitanju Bolade Casel, Dr. Ysaye Maria Barnwell,
Carol Maillard, Aisha Kahlil and Dr. Bernice Johnson Reagon

Published by
Contemporary A Cappella Publishing
Southwest Harbor, ME

DEDICATION

This book is dedicated to our Ancestors and
to all those who have, through their songs, woven into being a fabric of
African-American spirituality, history, culture and activism,
and to all those who will, with that fabric, make garments in the future.

We wish to dedicate these songs to
the memory of Beatrice Wise Johnson,
Joy McLean Bosfield and Ed Love.

ACKNOWLEDGMENTS

We acknowledge the presence of the Most High in all things
and give thanks for making this book possible.
We thank our editors, Jessika Diamond and Don Gooding, and our publisher, Contemporary A Cappella Publishing,
for making this book a reality.

We are deeply appreciative of the care, and skilled
assistance provided by Gloria and John Burgess.

TABLE OF CONTENTS

FOREWORD

by Harry Belafonte

It is 1997 and as Sojourner probes the secrets of Mars and seeks to give us insights into the universal order of things, humankind is encouraged by this technological phenomenon, examining the meaning of existence. For certain, no matter what is discovered that will tell us of things past and things to come, it must all be measured against its impact on human life, thought and development.

That the scientists have called this probe Sojourner, named after the great Black woman abolitionist Sojourner Truth, says much about what these scientists see as their mission. They seek to release us from the bondage of ignorance that stultifies our intellectual growth and understanding of our relationship to the greater order of things, in much the same way that Sojourner Truth sought to release us from the bondage of ignorance that caused one set of human beings to cruelly enslave another, denying us all the ability to embrace a deeper understanding of who we are and of our dependency on each other.

I have always believed art is the conscience of the human soul and that artists have the responsibility not only to show life as it is but to show life as it should be. Herein lies what is central to the power and the glory of Sweet Honey In The Rock. These women, the tribal and spiritual descendants of Sojourner Truth, have always understood their mission and, in their utterances, have consistently repelled the enemies of truth and helped immeasurably in giving us access to the celebration of our being.

On a recent visit to Central America, as my wife Julie and I moved through the wondrous unfolding of the rain forest and immersed ourselves in the life of the indigenous people of the region, I was deeply struck by what mankind's greed and ignorance have done in its cruel destruction of the forest and its people. I was reminded of Sweet Honey In The Rock's "Are My Hands Clean?" and had to ask myself in the face of this encounter, "are *my* hands clean?"

In 1994, as I traveled through the country of Rwanda, nestled in central Africa, and observed the aftermath of the devastating genocidal slaughter of 500,000 men, women and children, Hutu against Tutsi, I was again reminded of Sweet Honey In The Rock and recalled her song "Chile, Your Waters Run Red Through Soweto."

In Appalachia I listened to a White woman of no means speak of her coal miner husband, unemployed for seven years and a victim of black lung disease, and of their five children who will inherit the national debt. I reflected on "More Than a Paycheck" and "Ode To The International Debt." The strength of a song, the insightfulness of art!

Sweet Honey In The Rock's mission is not just to entertain, which she so admirably does, but also to open the mind and heart to thoughts about who we are and what we do to one another and to our fellow creatures. In so doing, she helps us find the courage to commit ourselves to the betterment of all life.

The richness of cultures past and present and all their glorious diversity has been seriously contaminated, and much of them sit on the brink of extinction. They limply grope for ways to resist the onslaught of the forces of profit that has set the scene for the decline.

Most artists do very little to defend the realm. Each generation seems to care less and less about cultural values. The quest for material power and the self-anointing that is lock-step with that quest and what we are prepared to morally surrender are central to the demise. And we are all caught up in this turmoil. The gods of profit do not serve justice, for they are unjust. They have no ethics or moral regard for what they deem expendable, whether it be culture, the rainforest or people. Our only hope is to examine this fact and develop the will and courage to reverse the trend.

For a quarter of a century, Sweet Honey In The Rock has withstood the onslaught. She has been unprovoked by the 30 pieces of silver. Her songs lead us to the well of truth that nourishes the will and courage to stand strong. She is the keeper of the flame.

The songs gathered in this collection are no ordinary assemblage. They do not come from the hummable din of pop culture's Top 10 mindlessness. These songs draw upon much sterner stuff. After all, they are the songs of Sweet Honey In The Rock. And although they, too, are very hummable, their poetry awakens the stilled heart and sparks the mind to things and thoughts that give purpose. Their melodies make the soul sing.

If because of our ignorance our planet becomes like Mars, a dry barren mass, perhaps in some future time when another intelligence from some distant place sends its Sojourner to probe a desolate earth, the rock they would most need to know about would be Sweet Honey.

HARRY BELAFONTE *is an icon of American popular music. As a young boy, he lived in Jamaica, returning to New York City for high school. At age 17, he joined the United States Navy for a two-year stint. He then settled in New York, where he became involved in the American Negro Theatre and the Dramatic Workshop.*

His debut as a singer at the Village Vanguard led to his first recording contract with RCA Victor and two film appearances: Bright Road *and* Carmen Jones. *His 1955 recording,* Calypso, *was the first pop album to sell one million copies. Mr. Belafonte has starred in the films* Buck and the Preacher *(1972) and* Uptown Saturday Night *(1974). He is a humanitarian and political activist who played a key role in the Civil Rights Movement, mobilizing the international arts community in support of the movement. He is the recipient of numerous awards and honors, including the first Nelson Mandela Courage Award.*

INTRODUCTION

by Horace Clarence Boyer

On February 28, 1927 in Memphis, Tennessee, the blind sanctified singer Mamie Forehand recorded a refrain based on Psalm 81:16. In this passage of scripture the poet and musician King David advised his people that if they would serve the Lord they would be rewarded by being fed "honey out of the rock," the place where according to legend of that time, the sweetest nectar was produced. The song became widely popular among Pentecostal, Baptist and Methodist congregations but, as often happens, it underwent a slight textual change on its way to popularity. While Forehand titled her song "Honey In The Rock" and sang those words, random congregations soon added the adjective "sweet" to the title, and the song has come down through history as "Sweet Honey in the Rock."

Forty-six years after Forehand introduced the song, a quintet of African-American women, singing as a unit of the vocal workshop of Washington D.C.'s Black Repertory Theater Company, organized an a cappella group and called themselves "Sweet Honey In The Rock." It would not overstate the case to add the overworked — but definitely applicable — phrase "and the rest is history."

The Ward Singers

A female a cappella group was a strange sight and sound in 1973. This in itself seemed strange, for female singing groups have been a part of African-American musical history since the first quarter of the 20th century, when African-American male a cappella groups were organized. But the groups remembered and written about have been the piano-accompanied groups such as The Hyers Sisters, The Ward Singers, The Shirelles and En Vogue. Completely forgotten are the trail blazers, among whom were the powerful Virginia Female Singers, whose 1921 recording of "Lover of the Lord" has recently resurfaced. Little-known facts that have surfaced about this group and others that followed are that they used the voice classification of the male quartets (tenor, bass, etc.) and arranged their own songs. Moreover the bass for the group could compete, without a handicap, with the bass of any of the male groups, including the famous Blue Jay Singers and the Birmingham Jubilee Singers.

Long forgotten are The Southern Harps, organized in New Orleans in 1935 and whose 1942 group was comprised of a lead, swing lead, alternate lead, tenor, baritone and bass. Of particular interest is the fact that the lead was Bessie Griffin, who, in the 1950's, would emerge as a gospel superstar, while the tenor was Helen Matthews, featured in the 1970's Broadway musical "Purlie" under the name Linda Hopkins. Their hometown compatriots were the Jackson Singers, organized in 1936, a group that produced a sound not unlike The Southern Harps, with whom they were often paired in concerts.

Also forgotten are the Golden Stars of Memphis, organized in 1938, as well as the more famous Songbirds of the South, organized in the same city in 1940. Fortunately one of its members, Cassietta George, made a significant musical contribution as a member of The Caravans.

Albertina Walker and The Caravans

Indeed the African-American a cappella quartet or quintet was created during the last half of the 19th century, and became a staple of American minstrelsy. It came into modern entertainment in 1905 when Fisk University, realizing it was too costly to send out their large group of Jubilee Singers, dispatched a quartet to replace them. African-American colleges and universities throughout the nation quickly organized similar groups, which inspired a battalion of Jubilee Singers in Birmingham and Bessemer, Alabama, in the second decade of the 20th century. Beginning with the organization of The Foster Singers in 1915, quartets of Jubilee Singers sprang up around the nation. The Fairfield Four were organized in 1921, The Dixie Hummingbirds in 1928, and these groups, in turn, inspired the organization of such secular music groups as The Mills Brothers in 1922, The Ink Spots in 1934 and The Delta Rhythm Boys in 1935. Sweet Honey In The Rock thus joined one of the most prestigious companies of music makers in the history of the United States.

The Dixie Hummingbirds

SWEET HONEY IN THE ROCK AND THE AFRICAN-AMERICAN A CAPPELLA SINGING TRADITION

Sweet Honey In The Rock is uniquely distinct from all of these groups. She is even different from Mamie Forehand, though, like Forehand and these groups, she makes melody, harmony, rhythm and message. And therein lies her unique quality: more than any group on the music scene today, "Sweet Honey" — as the group is affectionately called — carries a message. Absent from the group's songs are the moon and June rhymes, the pretty melodies with senseless words and any sign of the slightest fear of topical subjects. In fact, Sweet Honey is known as the group that will go where no other singers will go, textually.

At a concert of Sweet Honey, even before they open their mouths to sing, one is struck by the elegant, and yes, beautiful attire of the singers. Clad in colorful dresses of the finest African and eastern fabric, their heads are covered with striking (and intricately wrapped) turbans, or their hair is braided into elaborate designs adorned with ribbons and scarves. The singers grandly — and with a purpose — make their way to a group of chairs assembled in a semi-circle on stage and take their seats. Glancing briefly at each other they burst into sound, a sound unlike any heard in many years. As often as not they accompany themselves on rattles, gourds or sticks. The sound is that of sisters sitting around the fireplace singing songs of social commentary, a female choir in rehearsal, a congregation of Wednesday evening Prayer Services singers, or a village that has come together to sing through happiness, trials or death. Even as the melodies, harmonies and rhythms soar, one is immediately struck by the message of the songs, for the message is what Sweet Honey is all about.

In writing about Sweet Honey in Epic Lives – One Hundred Black Women Who Made a Difference (Visible Ink Press, 1993), Jesse Carney Smith notes "despite their name, which comes from a gospel song, Sweet Honey In The Rock's message is more often political (and social) than religious." "I think everything is political," (member Bernice Johnson) Reagon stated in People Magazine. "We are about being accountable." To be sure, Sweet Honey has become the surrogate conscience of the United States in that her songs will not let us rest while there is still work to be done. Indeed the topics of the songs range from the controversial Joanne Little case to the instructively ceremonial "Seven Principles," detailing, in English and Swahili, the principles of Kwanzaa. And the message is delivered without hostility or rancor but with the care of a friend and concerned loved one.

As the words of the songs become intense, Sweet Honey accents the meaning through a time-honored African-American practice of standing up and singing. The audiences, more than often, accept this as a sign for them, too, to show their involvement. They, too, stand, clap their hands and sway to the music. Before long the concert has turned into an ecstatic community revival. And clearly Sweet Honey is the leader of the revival. Just as clearly, the group is the Greek chorus, minstrels or community singers of our society, commenting on all matters of importance to the populace.

They are more than just community singers. These women, unlike the jubilee quartets of the 1920s, are not simply singers who, for lack of preparation or want of something else to do, or to make a living and contribution at the same time, fell into a singing group. They are educated (the group contains two members with earned Ph.D. degrees) and professional women who have accepted the charge of reminding us that we are all God's children. They have taken their songs and message not only throughout the United States and Africa but throughout Mexico, Germany, Australia, Japan, England and Russia, among many nations.

However, their position as community singers is important when it is realized that Sweet Honey almost single-handedly kept the a cappella group tradition alive until 1988 when Take 6 joined them in what is perceived as a revival of the a cappella group. Happily, today there is a plethora of such groups, many of which, both male and female, were inspired to organize by Sweet Honey. In yet another unique move, Sweet Honey includes in her concerts sign-language interpretation for the Deaf and hard of hearing, a practice begun by the group in 1979.

THE MUSICAL STYLES OF SWEET HONEY IN THE ROCK

While there is no doubt the uniqueness of Sweet Honey is the message, her musical sound is what attracts first-time listeners. Described in the magazine High Fidelity as breathtaking excursions into harmony singing and neck-hair raising in Downbeat, one is startled at the many musical guises through which the message may appear. At one time the message comes in the form of a low-down blues; at another it is presented through the 19th century Negro Spiritual; then as the song of a field worker or a chain-gang member; now as a mother singing a sweet lullaby to her child; often as ceremonial African chant with all of its rhythmic/melodic motives that border on becoming a mantra; again as a reggae song steeped in African punctuated rhythms; now as a rousing gospel song with congregational responses; or as a children's song, with rhythms that crave a ring play.

Regardless of the guise through which the message is presented, the Sweet Honey sound dresses it in splendid attire. In her singing, the four- and five-part harmony sounds as spontaneous as friends meeting on the street corner, though it has the refinement of a conservatory ensemble. The richness of the individual voices and the natural vibrato, huskiness, and agility that they innately possess is a trademark of the group. Placing the high voices in their middle register forces the bass (yes, there are two in the group) to its lower register, creating a sound of substance and body. Like the sweet singing quartets of old, Sweet Honey celebrates close harmony, precise attacks and releases, and understated — yet firm — rhythmic accentuation. At a moment's notice she can easily change to energetic and extremely intense solo and background singing, a preaching style of delivery, and the exaggerated rhythms of the hard-singing quartets.

The style for which Sweet Honey is most noted is the layered or polyphonic practice reminiscent of West African singing. In this practice the bass sets up a two- or four-bar motif (or ostinato) that not only sets the rhythmic base, but also the harmonic foundation. After several statements of this ostinato, a tenor or baritone enters with a contrasting motif that sets up a dual rhythmic and harmonic progression. On top of this, two other voices, perhaps a tenor and baritone or two tenors, add yet another contrasting motif and together the voices create a sonorous arabesque of harmony and rhythm that is as intricately designed as a tennis match is active.

At the moment that the listener thinks she or he has been exposed to all of the material of the song, the lead enters with a soaring melody that, because it is totally different from the sounds already presented, can gallantly ride on top of the harmony and rhythm set up by what has become the response to a call. This practice is so effective because the message of the leader is all the more pronounced as it sits atop a mountain of sound.

Another Sweet Honey device is the folk choral response composed of a single statement presented in perpetual motion behind the soloists. This device, created by the Tidewater Jubilee Quartets, involves setting up a textual or neutral syllable response such as oom-ma-lank-a-lank-a-lank over which the leader/soloist weaves a story. Another favored device is the classic response wherein the background singers repeat the leader's call, answer questions posed by the lead or complete statements begun by the lead. A favorite example of this device is found in W. Herbert Brewster's "Old Land Mark" in which the leader begins a statement with 'let us all go back' while the response states a diminished repetition, 'all go back.' The leader continues the statement with 'back to the old,' while the background singers complete the statement with 'old land mark.' Acknowledging the ingenuity of Sweet Honey, one can expect endless variations on all of these devices.

As if the use of the several devices at their command were not enough to provide variety in sound and technique, each member of Sweet Honey is a soloist in her own right and will lead one or two songs in each concert. This differs from such perennially single-soloist lead groups as The Supremes, where Diana Ross was the lead singer, and Martha and The Vandellas. Sweet Honey works in the tradition of such groups as The Roberta Martin Singers and The Caravans, groups in which each singer was also a soloist.

Eugene Smith, Archie Dennis, Delois Barrett, Roberta Martin and Gloria Griffen as the Roberta Martin Singers

SONGS IN THE COLLECTION

Over the 25 years of her existence, there have been many personnel changes within Sweet Honey In The Rock, but not changes in the distinctive style, sound and message. Of course as new members came into the group, each brought her special musical talent, resulting in an expanded palette from which the group could paint. For example, when Aisha Kahlil joined the group she brought a refined sense of jazz and improvisation; the entrance of Nitanju Bolade Casel signaled the addition of traditional West African vocal styles and rap. The new material was incorporated into the Sweet Honey style but their sound is still easily recognizable. The present group includes Ysaye M. Barnwell, Nitanju Bolade Casel, Aisha Kahlil, Carol Maillard and founder Bernice Johnson Reagon. This collection, CONTINUUM: The First Song Book of Sweet Honey In The Rock, is as unusual as the group in that each of the five singing members has contributed three original compositions and one traditional song arrangement. The songs are presented in choral score for easy use by vocal ensembles.

As might be expected, the songs in the collection fall into several categories by textual theme and style. The largest category, by theme, is that of social consciousness, dealing with several facets of the term. Within this category, five songs address the matter of freedom. Three of these are from the era of American slavery and speak to individual physical enslavement, while one song is concerned with the issue of contemporary freedom from the abundant social ills that plague our society.

The Negro Spiritual "No More Auction Block For Me," reportedly the inspiration for Charles Albert Tindley's "I'll Overcome Some Day," (which, in turn, inspired the creation of the Civil Rights anthem "We Shall Overcome") receives a much more lively arrangement than has surfaced before (Reagon). Sung on the day of The Emancipation Proclamation, the song declares that the days of selling Black people like cattle were over, though those who had died in slavery or ran away or were killed by slave owners or overseers would miss the celebration, for they were among the "many thousands gone." The transportation of Africans from their homeland for the purpose of slavery, leaving them "a long way from home" and therefore "without a mother" is the theme of "Motherless Chil'" (Maillard). Sensitively set as a community sing-along, this Negro Spiritual is given new life. Likewise, the Negro Spiritual "Cum Ba Yah" (Barnwell), or "Come By Here," implores the Lord, as He did with Daniel, to "deliver" them.

"Ella's Song" (Reagon) is the fourth song in the category of social consciousness - freedom songs. Based on the words of Ella J. Baker (1903-1986), one of the principal activists of the Civil Rights Movement of the 1960's, this is probably the most interesting song in the collection for it speaks directly to the killing of Black men ("until the killing of Black men... is as important as the killing of White men") and "passing on to others that which was passed on to me." Until such freedom is exercised throughout the world, "we cannot rest." Set in the conventional Negro Spiritual-type refrain, complete with folk harmonies (I, IV and V), this very moving arrangement captures Sweet Honey in her essence.

Respect, an important feature of social consciousness, is represented by two songs: "Young and Positive" (Casel) and "We Are" (Barnwell). The first of these songs, set as a rap with a rhythmic-tuned background, pays homage to the cultural diversity of America and declares this with the line "I don't want everybody to be like me." "We Are," arranged like an anthem of pride, solicits respect for the singers, declaring that they are "the builders of nations" and "a grandmother's prayer and a grandfather's dream." Our responsibility toward social consciousness is illustrated in its highest form in the exotic anthem, "Would You Harbor Me?" (Barnwell). The question of "Am I my brother's — or sister's — keeper?" is answered once and for all with a question: "Would you harbor me?" The answer is suggested in the composition, for the song begins with a solo voice. Another voice enters and a semi-chromatic harmony is added; then the song unfolds into full harmony (would you harbor a poet... king... slave... prophet... me?). The harmony represents all of God's children coming together to protect one another.

Some indication of the range of subjects is given in the song about spousal abuse, "Run" (Casel). Although this song deals with that most unspeakable injustice of physical abuse against the female partner (wife or lover), the song is definitely about such abuse against anyone. It is all the more poignant in this song as the lyricist declares that "no one has the right to hurt me. Especially when they say they love me." Fortunately for the listener and singer, the lyricist concludes that she will "run for my life before it comes to an end." This determination is solidified in the setting: not one of pity and fear, but one set to a rousing tempo, accompanied by hand drums. Sweet Honey is simply being herself in this composition.

The subject of commitment is an important one in the collection and is represented by four songs. Perhaps the most interesting of these is "I Remember, I Believe" (Reagon), a commitment to remembering the past. Set in 4/4 time in the major mode, the soloist rehearses the many questions of life ("I don't know how my people survived slavery"), but resolves them at the end of each refrain through the realization that she is alive and doing well in the statement "I remember, I believe." A more direct sense of the theme is covered in "Breaths" (Barnwell), a commitment to the continuation of life after death. Over a rolling arpeggio-like ostinato in the bass, accompanied by a multilayered harmonic and rhythmic foundation, the soloist shows her respect for — and commitment to — life in such lines as "those who have died have never, never left... they are in the rustling trees." "Prayer To The One" (Maillard), set in 4/4 meter and one of the few songs in the collection with a reference to the minor mode, pays homage to God, or the spirit, in a refrain of "Glory / Be thine / All space / Divine." In "Sometime" (Reagon), written in 6/8 meter in the major mode, the soloist delivers a litany of commitments to a partner (a wedding song) and notes that when they are together "shackles fall from her heart." The final song in the category, "Inner Voices" (Casel) in 4/4 meter with a bass ostinato, speaks to God in thanks for "keeping my life in tune / with the melody of the sun / and the harmony of the moon."

A collection such as this would be incomplete without addressing the subject of love, and two such songs are included. The most rousing of these is "Goin' To See My Baby" (Maillard).

In the major mode and 4/4 meter, the soloist virtually shouts "I don't care how I get there, but I gotta make this journey," while the background serves as the airplane, train or bus on which she travels. The very passionate "Stay" (Maillard) has the soloist declaring "when I'm with you, baby, not a word needs to be said." This is delivered in the doo-wop style, complete with the 4/4 time and major mode found in the style when it made its appearance in the 1960's.

The final category of songs in the collection is chants. Kahlil composed three of the five chants and has given a different character to each of them. Though each is set in 4/4 meter with multilayered ostinati, "Fulani Chant," "Dream Song of Love" and "Wodaabe Nights" each evoke a different sensation. "Alunde," arranged by Kahlil, is a traditional chant imbued with energy, power and the characteristic ostinato. "Denko" (Casel), composed in the "call and response" style, begins as a slow incantation and suddenly switches to an energetic shout tempo, with shekeres and other percussive rhythm instruments serving as accompaniment.

Since her organization, music lovers have attempted to sing the songs of Sweet Honey In The Rock. They can now take pleasure in the fact that the songs are available in music manuscript, complete with all the moving lines, glorious harmonies, and beloved rhythms. Enjoy!

PHOTO BY SHARON FARMER

Sweet Honey In The Rock

HORACE CLARENCE BOYER, *a graduate of Bethune-Cookman College and the Eastman School of Music, has been a professor of music at the University of Massachusetts at Amherst since 1973. He has served as a guest curator for the Smithsonian Institution and as a United Negro College Fund Distinguished Scholar-at-Large at Fisk University. A gospel singer, pianist and composer, Dr. Boyer recently edited* Lift Every Voice and Sing: An African-American Hymnal *for the Episcopal Church, and is the author of* How Sweet The Sound, The Golden Age of Gospel.

SWEET HONEY IN THE ROCK: HER-STORY
by Carol Maillard

In the early 1970's, television actor Robert Hooks started a professional acting company for Black performers in his hometown of Washington, D.C. It was called the D.C. Black Repertory Company and provided classes and workshops to aspiring professionals. Hooks wanted to be sure that everyone who participated in the workshops or joined the company would have more than the necessary skills to compete professionally in the world of performing arts. He wanted to be sure that the company had full knowledge and awareness of their culture and heritage. The talent that he and artistic director Van Whitfield gathered together was phenomenal. (I joined The Rep in 1972).

In addition to being able to act and move well, it was necessary for each actor to use her or his voice confidently whether speaking or singing, since the performance season included both traditional and experimental theatrical forms. Kenneth Daugherty and Charles Augins taught pantomime and dance, Van Whitfield sharpened skills through scene study, improvisation and acting classes, and Bernice Johnson Reagon was called in to train the voices. The actors also taught, built sets, designed costumes, handled lights and sound and learned to stage manage. All of these experiences gave them the skills to work both on and off stage.

Bernice brought a wealth of personal and professional experience to her classes at The Rep. The daughter of a Baptist minister from Albany, Georgia, Bernice grew up with the rich vocal traditions of Southwest Georgia. As a former member of the Student Non-Violent Coordinating Committee (SNCC) Freedom Singers and the Harambee Singers, Bernice's participation in the Civil Rights Movement is legendary. Her workshops at The Rep were filled with Spirituals, sacred music from the Black Church, songs from the Movement, work songs, children's songs, and love songs expressed in blues, jazz and R&B. She gave us everything that she had to stretch and strengthen us. And she was quite a disciplinarian. Many of the songs found their way to the stage and were powerfully delivered by the strongest singers. Some of the productions used instruments but most were done with a natural, a cappella sound. It was a brilliantly creative time at the Last Colony Theater, home of The Rep in Northwest Washington, D.C.

Two of the strongest performers, Louise Robinson and Le Tari, wanted to see if the music we were creating could do well in a concert setting and began to talk to Bernice about forming a vocal ensemble composed of the best singers at The Rep. Le Tari really persisted and was so enthusiastic about the idea that Bernice finally agreed to call the first rehearsal and the singers agreed to give it a try.

When the first meeting was called, the small rehearsal space next to the theater was filled with about a dozen singers - male and female, soprano to deep bass. Everyone was excited and ready to sing. One of the first songs Bernice offered was the song that eventually became the name of the group, "Sweet Honey In The Rock."

Sweet honey in the rock
Sweet honey in the rock
Know it tastes like honey in the rock
Sweet honey in the rock

During the summer of 1973, many of the singers took on other responsibilities and jobs until the fall schedule was put in place. Because of the theater's "hiatus," rehearsals with the full ensemble were difficult. Consequently, the original combination of singers never made it to performance as Sweet Honey In The Rock. The final mix of Bernice Reagon, Mie Fredericks, Louise Robinson and Carol Maillard happened by "divine intent."

After the summer season of 1973 ended, Bernice called a rehearsal and the three singers who saw the notice showed up. Bernice admits she was disappointed. She felt she didn't have a group. Louise remembers offering words of encouragement since she was confident that four voices would do just fine. And they did. Every song Bernice called was in full harmony, and the blend of voices was perfect. When she was scheduled to perform at the W.C. Handy Blues Festival at Howard University, Bernice told the coordinator of the program that she had a group that wanted to sing with her. The group debuted on November 17, 1973.

Remembering that first appearance as Sweet Honey In The Rock fills me with pride. All of the elements were there: strong and versatile voices, young women committed to honoring African-American culture, talented writers/arrangers and a fabulous sense of drama and stage presence. We were very excited to make that journey together. And now, 25 years later, all the elements are still there.

Since 1973, Sweet Honey In The Rock has touched the hearts, minds and souls of people worldwide. The thousands of faces, cultures, ages, lifestyles and beliefs that fill Sweet Honey's audiences are a living testimony to the power and universality of the group's music. From the D.C. Black Repertory Company and Howard University Sweet Honey has traveled to Beijing, Mexico City, Nairobi, Port Au Prince, Rio de Janeiro, Paris and cities all over the United States; to concert halls, political rallies and protest marches; to memorial services, nightclubs and festivals. Sweet Honey, as member Nitanju Bolade Casel wrote in her Rap song "A Tribute," "...is moving from continent to continent singing our songs, fightin' 'isms from a system pitting right against wrong." Audiences are encouraged to really listen to the songs and raise their voices, to take a stand and realize we all have more in common as human beings than the differences that tend to divide us. Virginia Giordano has said that "Sweet Honey always attracts the best people in the world." I agree.

Twenty-two women have offered their time, talent and skills to the sound and spirit that is Sweet Honey In The Rock. Whatever you hear on a recording or in live perfor-

mance contains the "DNA" of all the women who kept the group alive and growing. The DNA? I call it the Dynamic Nuances of our Ancestors. Each woman brings her own unique style of writing, arranging, storytelling, harmonizing and leading a song. This way, when a member has to leave for any reason, a new singer is accepted, not as a replacement for a particular voice, but as special and talented in her own right.

Although most of our songs were a cappella, Dianaruthe Wharton, a composition student at Howard University, was our pianist and we did several of her compositions when we performed. Our first recording (on Flying Fish Records) features Diana's "Shine On Me" and "Doin' Things Together." She also played piano accompaniment while I (Carol Maillard) played violin and Funches played bass on Bernice's "Hey Mann." After Diana moved to New York, Sweet Honey rearranged the tunes and continued to perform them a cappella.

Sweet Honey is a group that understands change and tries her best to work with every situation so that the group can continue. When Mie decided to move on in 1974, we held auditions and Evelyn (Evie) Maria Harris, a Howard University student, was selected as our new singer. During that time, three members of The Rep's acting company, Rosie Lee Hooks, Ayodele Harrington and Ingrid Ellis, also sang with Sweet Honey. In early 1975, Tia Juana Starks and Patricia (Pat) Johnson, both students at the University of The District of Columbia, worked with us for our Black History Month Performances at The Rep. Even with changes in the lineup, the sound of the group was always distinct, consistent and electric.

By the summer of 1975, Bernice Johnson Reagon, Louise Robinson and I were joined full time by Pat Johnson and Evelyn Harris. We brought in our original songs and sometimes did group arrangements (one of my favorites being "Moonshadow," recorded by LaBelle). We made strong appearances at the Mariposa Folk Festival in Toronto, the University of Chicago Folk Festival and on the African Diaspora Stages of the Smithsonian's Festival of American Folk Life.

Our first album was recorded and released in 1976 on the Flying Fish Label after Bruce Kaplan saw us in Chicago. From that first recording, Sweet Honey continued her relationship with Flying Fish until 1988, except for a Redwood Records Release of "B'lieve I'll Run On" in 1978.

When Louise decided to raise her daughter Asha in the Virgin Islands, another Rep member, Yasmeen Williams, became part of the group. I remember singing with her in Kentucky at Berea College in 1977. She sang Bernice's "My Way" with such compassion that I lost my place in the song and felt myself soaring with her. Over the years, Yasmeen's contribution as a song stylist, composer and arranger made an extraordinary impact on Sweet Honey's sound.

In 1977 I left Sweet Honey to pursue my acting career in New York, but continued to perform with Bernice, Yasmeen, Pat and Evie whenever it was possible. That became a challenge once I really started working a lot and the group toured California with singer Laura Sharpe. Sweet Honey was first booked by Ernestine Potter and then by Amy Horowitz, whose booking activities evolved into the organization Roadwork, Inc. Roadwork booked Sweet Honey for more than a decade and, in addition to the SisterFire Festival and a number of other events, produced many of Sweet Honey's anniversary concerts in Washington, D.C.

The summer of 1978 brought another tour of California. One of the highlights of that tour was a memorable performance at the Inner City Cultural Center of Los Angeles when Beah Richards, the well-known African-American actress, began the evening with a powerful presentation of poetry. Inspired, Sweet Honey completed the evening gloriously. This tour solidified Sweet Honey's loyal audiences in that state. In that same year, Sweet Honey recorded "B'lieve I'll Run On, See What The End's Gonna Be" on the Redwood Records label with Evie, Pat, Bernice and Yasmeen. Evie, Bernice and Yasmeen also participated in Bernice Johnson Reagon's soundtrack for the film *Wilmington 10, USA 10,000*, singing Bernice's compositions "Biko," "Cape Fear River" and "Echo."

Tulani Jordan(-Kinard) joined in 1978 when Pat retired from the group. And Bernice's heeding of an inner voice that told her to visit All Souls Church one Sunday resulted in Ysaye Maria Barnwell's joining in 1979. Ysaye was singing that Sunday and using Sign Language, simultaneously making her song and the message available to both hearing and non-hearing congregants. She became Sweet Honey's first interpreter when she performed at the 6th Anniversary Concert that year, but then continued as a singing member of the group after introducing Shirley Childress Johnson (Saxton), Sweet Honey's American Sign Language Interpreter since 1980. Shirley, born to Deaf parents, is a certified, professional interpreter who makes visible much of what our concerts are — energy, message, rhythm and movement — and heightens the hearing audiences awareness of Deaf language, culture and community.

Ysaye's deep, rich bass voice gives Sweet Honey a luscious cushion as well as a pulsing beat that often drives a song. In addition, she is a gifted composer and arranger with the ability to make any group of people sing and sing well. She has given exquisite melodies to poems including Kahlil Gibran's "On Children" and Birago Diop's "Breaths." These settings, as well as many of her compositions with original lyrics like "Wanting Memories," "Would You Harbor Me?" and "We Are...," have been incorporated into rituals from birth to death in communities around the world. "Breaths" has been choreographed by a number of people, sung by classmates at the memorial services of their teenaged friends, used during countless funerals and memorial services of persons who have died with AIDS and cancer and found its way into the four-part PBS series called "Living Positively," produced by AIDS FILMS. This song has been translated into the Maori language and was part of the soundtrack in a film developed by the German army to train soldiers on issues of death and dying. "Would You Harbor Me?" was used by a social worker to facilitate structured discussion among co-workers on the subject of acceptance and tolerance, and will be used as the basis for a three-day workshop on diversity.

In 1980, early Sweet Honey welcomed Helena Coleman and Geraldine Hardin into the group. Helena became pregnant with twins in the year, but managed to get through the First Black History Month Tour, Vancouver Folk Festival and No Nukes Day. Geraldine came in for Sweet Honey's first tour of Japan in December of the same year.

Sweet Honey's third album, "Good News," was recorded live at All Souls Church, Unitarian in Washington, D.C. in 1980 and released on Flying Fish in 1981. Aisha Kahlil joined Sweet Honey In The Rock in that year, introduced by Evelyn Harris who discovered, during a casual conversation, that Aisha was a singer looking for work because a job had just fallen through. Evie invited Aisha to come to a Sweet Honey workshop to learn the songs being taught and rehearsed and to see how things would work out. At that time, there was an opening for a new singer and Aisha became Sweet Honey's 19th member. Aisha brought her energy as a dancer and actress and her gift for improvisation to the performance stage. She encouraged the group to incorporate movement into the concerts. Aisha was on stage with Evie, Bernice, Ysaye, Yasmeen and Shirley for the 8th Anniversary Concert in Washington, D.C.

Michelle Parkerson, a Washington, D.C.-based African-American filmmaker, produced a film about Sweet Honey called "Gotta Make This Journey," which was broadcast on PBS in 1983 during our 10th Anniversary year. And what a year that was! The 10th anniversary album, "We All... Everyone of Us," produced by Evelyn Harris, contained some of the most powerful and poignant songs of struggle and triumph from the group. "Azanian Freedom Song" (Crying For Freedom) (Reagon), "Battle For My Life " (Harris) and "I'm Gon' Stand" (Reagon) were rallying cries to never forget the pain and suffering of South African Blacks under Apartheid, to fight racism, sexism and all forms of exploitation worldwide.

A magnificent and memorable 10th Anniversary celebration took place in Washington, D.C. in 1983. Roadwork produced a three-day concert series: a different concert each night at the University of the District of Columbia Auditorium, sung by 15 of the 19 women who had graced a Sweet Honey stage since 1973. We came together, full of the strength and energy that gave birth to the group and sustained her for all those years. We came back to give thanks and praise. We came back to give our love and support for Sweet Honey's future.

Since the 10th Anniversary extravaganza, we have celebrated the completion of each year with east coast concerts in Boston, New York and Washington, D.C, with gratitude, joy, reflection, courage and vision. Our fans are there full force to celebrate with us and they are in the audience in good voice and fine style. Some of them travel cross-country to be with us and we love to see their faces.

No two Sweet Honey concerts are ever alike. Since 1985, each member has been challenged with the opportunity to "program" performances. We each have our own style of structuring our list of songs for an evening. We do it on a rotating basis, so that the concert offered in Oakland on any given night will be different from the one in Boston on the following night.

Aisha's sister, Nitanju Bolade Casel, took part in Sweet Honey's summer workshop in 1985 upon her return from almost four years in Senegal, West Africa. Nitanju, like Aisha, was an accomplished dancer and singer, and she brought a wealth of West African songs and chants to Sweet Honey. At the 12th Anniversary Concert in Washington, D.C., Bernice, Evie, Aisha, Yasmeen and Ysaye were joined on stage by Tulani and Nitanju, who took the baton passed to her by Yasmeen as she became Sweet Honey's newest member.

Two recordings were released that year. A collection of sacred songs entitled "Feel Something Drawing Me On" and a recording with our customary range of musical forms and subject matter, "The Other Side." Both albums embraced a breathtaking array of writing, arrangements and genres. Within the sacred, "Waters of Babylon" was taken from the Jamaican Rastafarian tradition, "Meyengo" from West Africa and "Feel Something Drawing Me On" from the African-American church. "The Other Side" introduced Aisha's powerful Blues style with "Stranger Blues," and Ysaye's setting of Waring Cuney's poem "No Images" addressed Black self-image in the context of western standards of beauty. This album was the first to be co-produced by Bernice and her daughter Toshi Reagon, a gifted singer/songwriter/musician in her own right.

Sweet Honey In The Rock was privileged to participate in a PBS Special Presentation in honor of the first federal observance of the Martin Luther King, Jr. holiday in 1986. "Martin Luther King, The Dream and the Drum" was produced by Ossie Davis and Ruby Dee. It featured "Letter To Martin," a poem by Sonia Sanchez set to music by Sweet Honey; "Beatitude," Jesus' Sermon on the Mount set to music by Bernice Johnson Reagon; and "Peace," a poem written by Paul Eluard and translated from the French by Walter Lowenfeld, set to music by Nitanju Bolade Casel. These songs became part of Sweet Honey's second live album, "Live At Carnegie Hall." This double album, produced by Steve Rathe, recorded in 1987 and released in 1988, brought the group her first Grammy nomination for Evelyn Harris' "State of Emergency," a searing indictment of the perpetual "state of emergency" in Apartheid South Africa. We received a Grammy that same year as part of a film and recording titled "A Vision Shared: Woodie Guthrie and Leadbelly."

For many years, people have shared with us the impact our songs have on their daily lives, particularly in raising their children. From birthing to nap time to history lesson, our music has soothed, stimulated and taught. Parents knew our concerts were "child and family friendly" and knew it was fine to bring the kids along. Now, these 'Sweet Honey babies' come to us after a concert and to tell us how they are raising their children with our music and to thank us for branching out into the world of children's music.

"All For Freedom" and "I Got Shoes" were both recorded on the Music For Little People label. "All For Freedom," produced by Bernice Johnson Reagon and released in 1989, received two awards and gave us the opportunity to reach out to important, younger audiences. Rap is used to tell young listeners about the shekere, a gourd covered with beads and used as a rhythm instrument. A call and response song, "Everybody Oughta Know," talks about freedom, justice, friendship and happiness, and "So Glad I'm Here" is a great participation song, one which we often use to open our children's concerts. Our second children's recording, "I Got Shoes," produced by Toshi Reagon with the assistance of Nitanju Bolade

Casel, further expanded our outreach to young people, and in a natural evolution, led us to new and wonderful arenas: to Sesame Street, Reading Rainbow and the videotaping of a children's concert performed at Glide Memorial Church, San Francisco, California in 1995. The video is called *Singing For Freedom: A Concert for the Child in All of Us.* It was first broadcast on PBS, then made commercially available that year.

In 1989, I came back to Sweet Honey as a substitute singer when the group traveled to Japan and Australia, and on her first United States Information Agency tour of Uganda, Namibia, Swaziland, Mozambique and Zimbabwe for three weeks in 1990. Tulani and Yasmeen served as substitutes that year as well.

Regardless of how long it has been since last singing with the group, there is a very basic feeling of familiarity with the styles of the songs being raised. Either they are a part of your spiritual upbringing, or your time with Sweet Honey put you in unforgettable closeness to the material. Even though I was most familiar with Bernice's style and I was a founding member of the ensemble, it was easy in many ways to sing with Ysaye, Nitanju and Aisha, but challenging in other ways. To sing in Sweet Honey, it is very important to be a good listener in addition to being able to hang loose within the structure of the songs. You have to anticipate that a song can take on new vitality right on the stage and you have to be ready, willing and able to take flight within it as well.

Our history is so connected to the fabric of world history and politics that the events of 1990 spoke to our commitment and dedication over the past two decades. When Nelson Mandela was released from prison and it was clear that changes were going to be taking place in South Africa, we rejoiced. During the many rallies that celebrated his freedom and his mission to rid South Africa of the evils of Apartheid, we sang our songs of support and gratitude - in New York's Yankee Stadium, in Washington, D.C. and in Oakland, California. We were also fortunate to meet and sing for Winnie Mandela at the Brooklyn Academy of Music during the Mandelas' U.S. tour.

We added another name to the many Sweet Honeys in 1991, when Akua Opokuwaa substituted for Shirley Childress Johnson (Saxton) as our Sign Language Interpreter for the entire year. Evie also returned to the group after a year-long hiatus.

Sweet Honey began her relationship with EarthBeat! Records with a recording produced by Bernice and Toshi Reagon – "In This Land." This release included Nitanju and Aisha's rap manifesto for women, "Women Should Be A Priority," and two very special compositions. The title song, "In This Land," written by Steve Langley, addresses issues of hunger, homelessness and poverty in this land of plenty called America. Michelle Lanchester recalls in "Patchwork Quilt" the overwhelming love and emotion she felt for the thousands of people who had died with AIDS and were being remembered at the first unfolding of the Names Quilt in Washington, D.C. When the song was written, it was a radical statement of love for a community of people who had been scorned and rebuked. It was also a tribute to the love and courage of the family members, friends and lovers who took a stand on their behalf.

I found myself back in Sweet Honey full time in 1992 as we made our way towards our 20th anniversary celebration. We wrote a book — We Who Believe in Freedom: Sweet Honey In The Rock — 20 Years and Still On The Journey (Edited by Bernice Johnson Reagon) — chronicling the 20 years of Sweet Honey's journey. The voices of group members, family, friends, producers and many of the people who made it possible for us to be together on and off stage for two decades were included. We were blessed with an introduction by Alice Walker. "Still On The Journey" was the title of the 20th anniversary recording, also co-produced by Bernice and Toshi, and we spent the entire year celebrating worldwide. Yes, we toured for all 12 months of the 1993/1994 season.

Much has happened since the year-long celebration of 1993. Another sacred music recording, "Sacred Ground," produced by Bernice Johnson Reagon, came out in 1995 with songs of love for God, healing, inner wisdom and compassion, and songs in gratitude for the power of the light within that leads us forward. A special, special recording.

Within the past five years, we have had some wonder-filled experiences: back to Australia; first-time concerts in Singapore and Hawaii in 1994; the 1995 International Conference of Women in Beijing, China (Non-Governmental Organizations Conference in Huariou); a tour of Brazil; a concert in Port-au-Prince, Haiti where Sweet Honey was the first international group to perform and to have an audience with her President, Jean Bertrand Aristide, following his return to that office; to England, France, Germany and Austria. In 1996 it was back to Australia and adding New Zealand to our favorite places.

When we've toured in Australia and New Zealand, we have had the good fortune to have incredible Aborigine and Maori artists begin the evening concert for us; among them, the Bangara Dance Company, Archie and Ruby Roach, Kev Carmody and Maroochi Baramba in Australia, and Moana Jackson in New Zealand. Whether they are dancers, singers, songwriters or musicians, they all echo the feelings we share about racism, equality, cultural pride and the resolve to be a catalyst for positive and constructive change for their people. We learned a lot from their stories and songs. Most importantly, we saw first-hand how the Civil Rights Movement in America affected their sense of identity and what they needed to do to mobilize themselves. It was reassuring to know that our struggles made a difference on the other side of the world. African-Americans need to know the degree to which our struggles have had an impact on people around the world.

As we move ahead into Sweet Honey's future, we take not only the voices of all the women who have sung on a Sweet Honey stage, but we also take the love of everyone who has supported us over the years. CONTINUUM is a part of our history now. We offer you these songs in a form that is unique for us, coming as we do from the oral tradition. Sing them, share them, make them your own. Speak the poems and let them live through you. As you spread the honey around, let others taste the sweetness and know the strength that is Sweet Honey In The Rock.

**ASHE, ASHE, ASHE...
TO OUR ANCESTORS...
TO THOSE AS YET UNBORN...**

PHOTO BY SHARON FARMER

NOTES ON PERFORMANCE

by Ysaye M. Barnwell

It has been said, and rightly so, that the quintessential Sweet Honey In The Rock experience is her live performance. It is a soul stirring experience – sweet and rock solid – like no other. The powerful voices of these five African-American women, combined with hand percussion instruments, hand-clapping and foot-patting, create a blend of lyrics, movement and narrative which relates history, points the finger of justice, encourages activism and sings the praises of love. They are dedicated to justice, encourages activism and sings the praises of love. They are dedicated to preserving, celebrating and extending African-American culture and singing traditions.

Most of the time when one is provided a score like the ones in this songbook, the goal is to study and express the music as it has been represented on the page. The performer brings her or his technical proficiency to the task, and the quality of their artistry is determined by the degree to which she or he can effectively and repeatedly deliver, to the audience, what is on the page. While we have here presented accurate transcriptions of the songs (as most of them appear on our recordings), it is important to understand that in the African-American tradition and in the experience of Sweet Honey, music evolves as it is performed. In that sense, these scores are a guide to a given performance of Sweet Honey In The Rock but may have little relationship to a Sweet Honey performance that might be experienced six months, a year, or two years later.

People often want to know how much of Sweet Honey's performance is rehearsed and how much is improvised in performance. It is difficult to answer *how much*; however, the following thoughts might be helpful.

Sweet Honey performs a wide range of musical forms, including traditional African chants and songs, spirituals, traditional and contemporary gospel, blues, jazz, reggae, rap, children's game songs, lullabies and (common, long and short) metered hymns. Each of these musical forms has its own set of rules with an harmonic system, a rhythmic structure and a preferred vocal placement. In many instances, the rules for singing these forms are learned by osmosis as one grows up in the culture that has created the form. Most of the 22 women who have been members of Sweet Honey have grown up in churches where spirituals, metered hymns and/or gospels were sung. As a result, when songs in these forms are brought to the group, there is a frame of reference for singing them.

Sweet Honey members teach each other and learn, using the traditional oral/aural method. *Call and response* is a fundamental part of this process and is a basic feature which can be found in most African-American song forms. In rehearsal, we establish who will sing the melody (which is not necessarily a solo lead line) and each of the harmony or rhythmic lines. We rehearse the song until all singers are comfortable with the form, the song, and her part. At this point the singer is free to sing the song, to let the song sing her, to let the song sing itself.

One should only begin to improvise when they are certain of the rules governing the musical form in which they are operating. The scale or improvised embellishments used in a jazz song may not be appropriate when singing gospel; likewise, those found in gospel may not be appropriate when singing spirituals in the traditional way. The melodic and harmonic structure of a metered hymn sung in Georgia may be very different from the same hymn "raised" in Virginia. The differences between and among forms, whether subtle or extreme, need to be acknowledged and observed nevertheless.

Generally, there is no requirement for a song to be sung in exactly the same way it was sung before. The goal in African-American culture is often to sing until the song sings itself or 'til spirit or the power of the "Lawd descends." In this context, the performer's technical proficiency includes degrees of risk taking and degrees of emotional and spiritual vulnerability not generally accepted in the performance of (for example) European classical music. This kind of performance is totally dependent upon the performer's willingness to listen - to the voices within and the voices outside of one's self.

It is especially important to listen and to be aware of how "your part" interacts with and relates to other parts. If one listens carefully, several things can happen: perhaps you will find that what has been a mechanical experience becomes fresh and exciting each time the song is sung; you might find yourself surprised, delighted and inspired by what other singers are doing, challenging you to respond in a creative way; perhaps you will allow yourself to respond to the emotional and spiritual intent of the song; perhaps as you find yourself more comfortable with the form you will begin to hear and entertain a number of options for making subtle changes in the rhythm and/or melody of your line as well as in its dynamics.

Someone once asked if anyone in Sweet Honey had perfect pitch. As far as I know, none of Sweet Honey's 20 singing members has possessed (or been possessed by) perfect pitch; in spite of this, we do not use a pitch pipe. It is not in our tradition to do so. Perplexed, the questioner pointed out that the consequence of not using a pitch pipe or providing a starting pitch was that Sweet Honey would never be able to begin a song together at the same time, or on a chord. True. It is not in this tradition to do so. Instead, songs are begun by a song leader who might change from song to song, and who pitches the song as she or he feels it. This is as common a practice in the African-American tradition as beginning a song together and on the same pitch each time is in the European classical tradition. While this process works remarkably well for congregations and for small ensembles like Sweet Honey, it may wreak havoc on, and is not necessarily recommended for, choirs.

A *song leader* is not necessarily the same as a solo lead singer in a song. A song leader opens a song and is joined almost immediately by the congregation or rest of the ensemble. Most often the song leader is singing the melody line. If the song is congregational, the leader may recede into the congregation until it is time to initiate a new verse or begin another song. Sometimes, however, the song leader may in fact be singing the 'lead' in a song which has the other voices in the background. The first lead may be taken over by a second lead, singing on another line. For example, a soprano or tenor lead in a quartet style song may be taken over by a bass lead, and, ultimately, the two voices may sing in a lead position together.

Rhythm is fundamental in African and African-American music. It is not uncommon to find layers of different rhythms all being performed at the same time. Often, it is through the layering of "poly-rhythms" that the melody is created. This is a very different experience from that of Western music, in which a single melody line can be performed from start to finish by a single voice. African-based and African-derived music, with its repeated rhythmic patterns, can be described as cyclical, while Western music can be described as linear. The power of repetitive rhythmic patterns is that they are both transforming and trance-formative for those who produce them and for those who experience them. Singers performing these kinds of rhythmic parts for the first time are inclined to become bored or frustrated if they don't understand the power and intensity of repetition or how their parts relate to each other to form a larger sound that none of the parts could create alone. Once you have learned your part, you are free to listen to the conversation between parts as well as to the larger sound or melody created. Rhythm parts must never lose their precision or their intensity, else the integrity of the composition will be compromised. These parts are the drum that was taken from us during slavery, the heartbeat and the foundation of the composition. Listening deeply can and will help keep those singing rhythmic lines alert and involved in the composition.

We hope that as you venture into performing the songs included in this volume, you will take advantage of the recorded materials as a reference and resource. In addition, we look forward to welcoming you to a live Sweet Honey performance. There is a difference. We hope you will be able to capture the essence of this difference in your performances as well.

PHOTO BY SHARON FARMER

INSTRUMENTATION USED BY SWEET HONEY IN THE ROCK

Although Sweet Honey In The Rock is an a cappella group, we do use some instrumentation to enhance the rhythm and texture of our music. The following is a brief description of some of the instruments we use.

CLAVES - percussion sticks (often made of rosewood), which are used widely in Latin American music. One stick is held across the palm of the left hand and is struck by the stick held with the fingers and thumb of the right hand.

SHEKERE - a gourd of almost any size that has been dried, hollowed out and dressed with a mesh of strung beads, which can produce a wide range of rhythms when shaken, twisted and thrown. They are used throughout Africa, Latin America and the United States.

SHAKERS - chicken eggs, rattles, shakers of all kinds.

RAIN STICKS - bamboo or wooden tubes of varying length (from 12 inches to six feet) that contain pellets which travel an obstacle course as they fall from the top to the bottom of the tube. The length of the tube and the complexity of the obstacle course results in a sound much like falling rain that can last for quite a few minutes before the stick must be turned so that the pellets can begin their fall again. Rain sticks can also be shaken for effect. Rain sticks typically come from South America.

SLIT DRUM - a percussion instrument (which can vary in size and the number of slits) made by cutting a slit or slits in the wall of a hollow log. The "lips" created by the slits can vary in length and/or thickness, producing different pitches when struck with a mallet or beater.

OCEAN DRUM - a thin, double-headed drum, 12-24 inches in diameter, containing pellets that roll freely inside the drum. When the direction and speed of the pellets is controlled by the player, the sound produced is very much like the roar of the ocean and the crashing of waves.

AUSTRALIAN CLAP STICKS - traditionally struck against the side of a didgeridoo as it is played, these sticks (which can vary in length from several inches to more than a foot) are often elaborately decorated with Aboriginal designs. We use them as claves and they produce a softer, more mellow sound.

TAMBOURINE - a small frame drum with paired metal disks loosely fitted into slots parallel to the head. A variety of exciting rhythms can be played on the tambourine by shaking, striking, rubbing it with your free hand and/or striking it against your body.

MARACAS - paired round or oval shaped rattles, one slightly higher in pitch than the other. They are shaken to create a rhythm. Maracas are commonly used in Latin American and Caribbean rhythms.

TAMBOURACA - a six-sided, closed plastic tube which looks like a headless (plastic) tambourine without its disks, and containing pellets which cause it to sound like maracas. This is a relatively new invention.

COWBELL - a large single bell without a clapper, which is struck with a stick to produce its sound.

DAWURU - iron castanet-type finger bells, in two pieces: one, a ring worn on the thumb and the other a rounded, hollow lemon-sized bell, which can be worn over the middle finger. The thumb ring strikes the larger rounded piece to produce a sharp bell sound. In Ghana, this type of bell is the leader of the drum orchestra because of its powerful piercing sound.

DOUBLE BELL (known by many different names) - two bells of forged iron usually fused together into one stem by which the instrument is held when played. The bells are pitched so that the top bell is the higher and the bottom the lower in pitch.

A SIGN INTERPRETER'S SONG

by Shirley Childress Saxton

The goal and responsibility of a Sign Language Interpreter is to facilitate communication between Deaf and Hearing people. This is most effectively achieved by using the language of the Deaf, which in the United States is American Sign Language (ASL).

For many Deaf people, music and singing are foreign media, and its relevance in their lives is debatable. Music is often perceived as another sound-based communication barrier, an instrument of discrimination and oppression of Hearing upon Deaf. So why would Deaf people be interested in a Sweet Honey In The Rock singing experience? Perhaps for some of the same reasons as Hearing people - to exult, celebrate and praise God, life and living, creativity and culture; to sing the blues or discuss politics; or maybe to share a good time with family members and friends. Each Deaf (and Hearing) person "hears" Sweet Honey differently. While the vocal harmonies may not register, a poignant message can leave a memorable impression.

The challenge of interpreting the songs of Sweet Honey In The Rock is to accurately convey the message of the songs, reflect the mood and emotional intent of the singers and render visually the melody, harmony and rhythm of the music. I accepted the challenge of interpreting Sweet Honey In The Rock's message and music in 1980, after having interpreted professionally for seven years. Sweet Honey In the Rock had, in that year, made a commitment to making concerts accessible to the Deaf and to developing a Deaf audience. From the beginning, the group included the Sign Language Interpreter in her costuming and in the semi-circle in which she sits or stands to perform. This inclusion has been a clear statement to the Deaf audience that they are included in the conversation.

Each song is an expression of the self. Each has a story line and personality. For example, in "Breaths" the tempo is slow, the attitude is spiritual, encouraging an open heart and mind. The first word is "Listen;" the first sign represents the concept of gaining one's attention. Interpretation may include information useful as a frame of reference. I indicate which singer is leading the song. Because all members of Sweet Honey In The Rock lead songs, the Deaf audience may not otherwise recognize who the leader is for a particular song. The signed interpretation of the song may also include relevant cultural and historical information, and broader identification and definition of concepts and vocabulary. In my use of American Sign Language, the interpretation of a song is not an exact word-to-sign translation, but a full and vibrant visual depiction of the message.

Sweet Honey's repertoire includes songs in languages other than English. "Denko," for example, is in the Bambara language of Mali, West Africa. I am not yet proficient in any of the African Sign Languages, so my interpretation focuses on an explanation of the song's origin and meaning with a spelling of some of the lyrics using American Sign Language.

Some songs, like "Fulani Chant," have no words at all. Here, the interpreter is challenged to visually represent the sounds being made — a moan, a hum, a breath, a brisk wind, an ocean wave, a complex rhythm or a singer's a cappella characterization of a musical instrument. I imagine an abstract painting using color and shape to create a picture. Thus a movement or gesture with grace or force, a fluctuation of the hand, arm or shoulder with patterns big and small may be used in combination with verbal descriptions to help visualize the sound. Each Sign Language Interpreter will have her or his own unique interpretive style. My style tends to be fluid, loosely scripted, not static. Vocabulary and movements may change from performance to performance as the lead singer may not sing a song the same way each time it is performed. As thoughts or concepts may be expressed using various word and musical choices, so, too, can American Sign Language use a selection of signs and/or phrases representing the same idea.

Determining that a signed interpretation of a song is "good" can be subjective as well as objective. One can assess the interpreter's comfort level, pacing, visual clarity, vibrancy of vocabulary and visually poetic presentation. Effectiveness also can be measured by the Deaf audiences' ease in understanding the message of the song. As Sweet Honey In The Rock opens her mouth to sing, the Sign Language Interpreter moves her hands to sign. As the lyrics exclaim their message and as the melodies, harmonies and rhythms are vocalized, they are paralleled by the poetry and power of the visual language of American Sign.

SHIRLEY CHILDRESS SAXTON *joined Sweet Honey In The Rock as Sign Language Interpreter in 1980. A veteran professional Sign Language Interpreter, she learned American Sign Language from her Deaf parents. Shirley has 20 years experience providing Sign interpreting services in a wide range of life situations, including employment, education, law, health and performing arts/music. She holds a Bachelor's degree in Deaf Education and is a certified member of the Registry of Interpreters for the Deaf, Inc. Shirley teaches Sign Language classes and conducts master workshops on interpreting music.*

YSAYE M. BARNWELL

BREATHS · WOULD YOU HARBOR ME?
WE ARE… · CUM BA YAH (TRAD./ARR.)

YSAYE M. BARNWELL, editor of this volume, is a native New Yorker now living in Washington, D.C., where, since 1979, she has performed with Sweet Honey In The Rock. She appears as a vocalist and/or instrumentalist on more than 20 recordings with Sweet Honey In The Rock as well as other artists. In addition to being a singer with a range of more than three octaves, Dr. Barnwell spends much of her time offstage educating the world as a master teacher and clinician in cultural performance theory and voice production. Her workshop, *Building a Vocal Community: Singing In The African-American Tradition*, has been conducted all over the United States, Great Britain and Australia, making her work in the field a real source of inspiration for her performances on stage. This workshop has been documented in an instructional boxed set of six tapes (or four CDs) and a manual with the same title, produced by Homespun Tapes, Woodstock, New York.

Daughter of a registered nurse and a violinist, her 15-year study of the violin began at age two. Dr. Barnwell holds the Bachelor and Master of Science degrees in Speech Pathology (SUNY, Geneseo), Doctor of Philosophy in Cranio-Facial Studies (University of Pittsburgh) and Master of Science in Public Health (Howard University, Washington, D.C.). She has been a professor at the College of Dentistry at Howard University, and in addition to conducting community-based projects in computer technology and in the arts, she has administered and implemented health programs at Children's Hospital National Medical Center and at Gallaudet University in Washington, D.C. In her first year with Sweet Honey, Barnwell provided leadership in developing the group's practice of making concerts accessible to the Deaf through Sign Language interpretation.

Since joining Sweet Honey In The Rock in 1979, she has composed and arranged music appearing on 11 recordings on the Flying Fish, EarthBeat!, Music For Little People and Rykodisc labels. She has been a commissioned composer on numerous and varied dance, choral, film and video projects, including Sesame Street, Dance Alloy of Pittsburgh, David Rousseve's Reality Dance Company, Liz Lerman Dance Exchange, Women's Philharmonic of San Francisco and Redwood Cultural Work - all outgrowths of her combined understanding of the creative artist inextricably bound to society. In 1996 she was awarded The Bessie Award for her score "Safe House: Still Looking," commissioned by Liz Lerman Dance Exchange. Her music, published by Barnwell's Notes Publishing, has been performed and recorded by choral ensembles as well as individual artists.

In addition to these endeavors, Dr. Barnwell is an aspiring actress whose credits include voice-over narration in several documentary films and videos, a principal role on the TV series *A Man Called Hawk*, and a brief appearance in the film *Beloved*, directed by Jonathan Demme.

BREATHS
LYRICS ADAPTED FROM THE POEM BY BIRAGO DIOP
MUSIC BY YSAYE M. BARNWELL

Listen more often to things, than to beings,
Listen more often to things, than to beings,
'Tis the ancestors' breath when the fire's voice is heard,
'Tis the ancestors' breath in the voice of the waters.

Those who have died have never, never left.
The dead are not under the earth.
They are in the rustling trees,
They are in the groaning woods,
They are in the crying grass,
They are in the moaning rocks.
The dead are not under the earth.

Listen more often to things, than to beings,
Listen more often to things, than to beings,
'Tis the ancestors' breath when the fire's voice is heard,
'Tis the ancestors' breath in the voice of the waters.

Those who have died have never, never left.
The dead have a pact with the living.
They are in the woman's breast,
They are in the wailing child,
They are with us in our homes,
They are with us in this crowd.
The dead have a pact with the living.

Listen more often to things, than to beings,
Listen more often to things, than to beings,
'Tis the ancestors' breath when the fire's voice is heard,
'Tis the ancestors' breath in the voice of the waters.

WOULD YOU HARBOR ME?

LYRICS AND MUSIC BY YSAYE M. BARNWELL

Would you harbor me? Would I harbor you?
Would you harbor me? Would I harbor you?

Would you harbor a Christian, a Muslim, a Jew?
a heretic, convict or spy?
Would you harbor a runaway woman or child,
a poet, a prophet, a king?
Would you harbor an exile or a refugee,
a person living with AIDS?
Would you harbor a Tubman, a Garrett, a Truth,
a fugitive or a slave?
Would you harbor a Haitian, Korean or Czech,
a lesbian or a gay?...

Would you harbor me? Would I harbor you?
Would you harbor me? Would I harbor you?

WE ARE...

LYRICS AND MUSIC BY YSAYE M. BARNWELL

For each child that's born,
a morning star rises
and sings to the universe
who we are.

We are our grandmothers' prayers,
We are our grandfathers' dreamings,
We are the breath of our ancestors,
We are the spirit of God.

We are
Mothers of courage,
Fathers of time,
Daughters of dust and
Sons of great vision,
Sisters of mercy and
Brothers of love,
Lovers of life and
Builders of nations,
Seekers of truth and
Keepers of faith,
Makers of peace and
the Wisdom of ages...

We are our grandmothers' prayers,
We are our grandfathers' dreamings,
We are the breath of our ancestors,
We are the spirit of God.

For each child that's born,
a morning star rises
and sings to the universe
who we are,

WE ARE ONE.

CUM BA YAH

TRAD. SPIRITUAL / ARR. BY YSAYE M. BARNWELL

Cum ba yah my Lord, cum ba yah
Cum ba yah my Lord, cum ba yah
Cum ba yah my Lord, cum ba yah
Oh Lord, Cum ba yah
Oh Lord, Cum ba yah
Oh Lord, Cum ba yah
Cum ba yah

Someone's singin' Lord, cum ba yah
Someone's singin' Lord, cum ba yah
Someone's singin' Lord, cum ba yah
Oh Lord, Cum ba yah
Oh Lord, Cum ba yah
Oh Lord, Cum ba yah
Cum ba yah

Someone needs you, Lord, cum ba yah
Someone needs you, Lord, cum ba yah
Someone needs you, Lord, cum ba yah
Oh Lord, Cum ba yah
Oh Lord, Cum ba yah
Oh Lord, Cum ba yah
Cum ba yah

COMPOSER'S NOTES

BREATHS

I first heard Birago Diop's poem "Breaths " read at a funeral in the early 1970s, and I never forgot the comfort and clarity it gave me. I have been pleased to hear that over the years, this song has been sung at many funerals and seems to have provided comfort to others as well.

In the African world view, the invisible world of spirit and man and the visible world of nature exist along a continuum and form an organic reality. The same is true of the relationship between past, present and future. In Birago Diop's poem "Breaths," we are reminded of this continuum.

In setting this poem, I have tried to create a continuous melody line, rhythms that represent the relationship between our very human rhythmic functions and the laws of nature and breath sounds representing the breath of life and the presence of spirit and air around us. The piece was originally written for Sweet Honey In The Rock, which in 1980 was composed of four women. The piece works well for small ensembles and full choir without instrumentation, and for solo voice with accompanying rhythm instruments.

Birago Diop was born in Dakar, Senegal in 1906 and worked as a veterinary surgeon in Upper Volta. He has authored a book of poetry called <u>Leurres et Lueurs</u> (<u>Lures and Gleams</u>), Presence Africaine, 1960. He has also published several books of African tales, which he translated into French: <u>Les Contes d'Amadou Koumba</u> (<u>Tales of Amadou Koumba</u>) and <u>Les Nouveaux Contes d'Amadou Koumba</u> (<u>New Tales of Amadou Koumba</u>), available from Panther Press (Box 3552, GCPO, NY, NY 10017), and <u>Contes Choisis</u> (<u>Selected Stories</u>), published by Cambridge University Press (NY, NY 1967).

WOULD YOU HARBOR ME?

In 1993, I was asked by Liz Lerman (Dance Exchange) to write music for a dance work (*Safe House: Still Looking*) that would explore contemporary experiences with the concept of safety from the historic perspective of the Underground Railroad. During the dance, slave narratives and contemporary narratives of the dancers were fused with those of members of the audience and community into a tapestry of experiences that formed a continuum of human struggle for freedom.

No matter what physical or social condition we find ourselves in, the struggle for freedom must be waged and won first and foremost within our own minds. That spiritual, psychological freedom gives us the courage to do what is necessary to wage the external struggles against the forces of oppression such as slavery, racism, sexism, homophobia, religiosity, fundamentalism, addictions, etc., which challenge each of our lives.

When slaves decided to escape to the physical freedom of the North, it was with the help of those who felt free enough that they could risk themselves to help, those who felt they could harbor those in need. Well, there are many in need today. Will I help you? Will my community receive you? Will you help me? Based on what values and circumstances do I determine who I will risk myself to help? From whom will I receive help?

"Would You Harbor Me" is very much a chant. The melody is a one-note drone that can be sung on a single note or enhanced by singing in two or three octaves. If you were to sing this without the score, you would maintain the drone and begin to vary that melody by sporadically moving a half or whole tone from the melody, then back. Next you could add harmony lines, on the third and fifth, that

also do not move very far from their base. It is as much a meditation for the singer(s) as a composition to be performed. It is a conversation being held among the singers, and between the singer(s) and the listener(s). Enunciation is very important. The final questions: "Would you harbor me? Would I harbor you?" should be a swirl of sound, a kind of canon set in motion on the harmony lines. The tempo does not vary until the slight ritard on the last statement.

WE ARE...

"We Are …" is the last song in a suite entitled "Lessons," which was commissioned by Redwood Cultural Work (Oakland, CA). The opening lyric says "…Lawd, it's a midnight without stars." This song completes the cycle "For each child that's born, a morning star rises…"

Every child born gives us renewed hope for the world, but for each child to know their value and understand their responsibility in the world, they must know who they are. And they must understand that the sum total of all the things we are is one. In all the ways that count, we are one.

"Lessons" was written for SATB chorus. The rhythmic patterns are cyclical and repeat throughout. It is wonderful when each rhythmic voice hears and feels its relationship to the other rhythms. The basses should work towards a blend and a tone quality that sounds like the double bass section of a symphony. All of the rhythms together should have a Swingle Singers-type sound. It is probably best that the litany of who we are be sung by a solo voice able to really deliver the lyric with appropriate melodic variations tending toward a jazz feel.

CUM BA YAH

I first remember hearing "Cum Ba Yah" when I was in college during the early 1960s. This song, along with "Michael Row The Boat Ashore," was very popular at hootenanies and among (mostly White) folk singers, and both songs found their way into the popular culture of the time. It was a few years before I learned/understood that these songs could be traced to Black people, living on the islands off the coasts of South Carolina and Georgia, who had retained many aspects of the African cultures they brought with them as slaves. Generally, this music was unaccompanied and much more rhythmic and harmonically intense than the popular version of these songs suggested – with their emphasis on melody, usually accompanied by guitar arpeggios. I began to wonder what this song would have sounded like during an earlier period of its existence.

The phrase "Cum Ba Yah" is a linguistic variant of "Come By Here."

This arrangement combines several musical elements that were common in the regions mentioned above: a frontal (nasalized) vocal placement, a call and response pattern and a strong rhythmic drive. The opening call is free form, as are the random but harmonized responses. After the opening call, an energetic rhythmic pattern begins. The traditional rhythm for this kind of song consists of heel and toe foot pats on 1 & 2 & 3 & 4 &, a pounded stick or set of claps on 1 - 2 - 3 - 4 and a set of syncopated claps on 1 - 2 & 3 - 4 & in which the claps on 2 and 4 occur slightly before the beat.

In the performance of the song, the song leader introduces reasons why she or he wishes the Lawd to come by here. After the initial statement, the reason is repeated by the congregation: people need you, someone's prayin', we need freedom, someone's singin', children hungry, people dyin', nations fightin', etc.

Breaths

Lyrics adapted from the poem by
Birago Diop

Music by Ysaye M. Barnwell

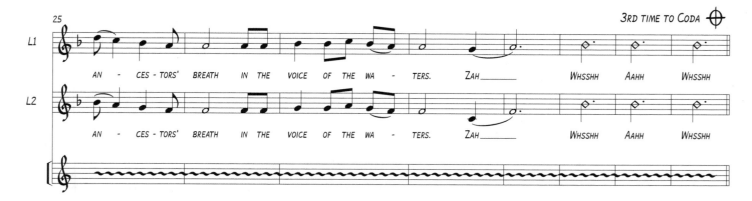

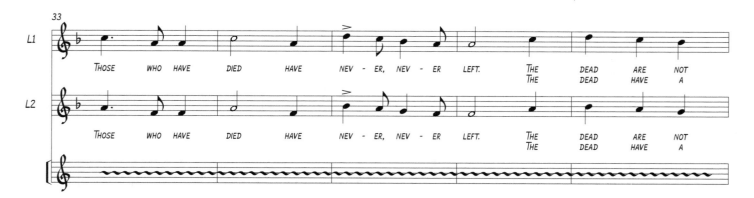

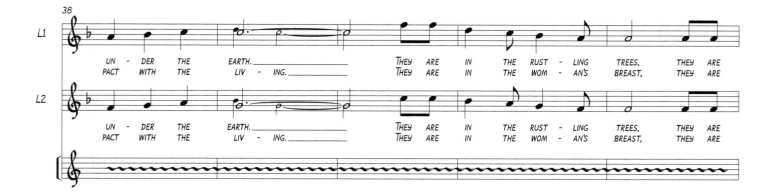

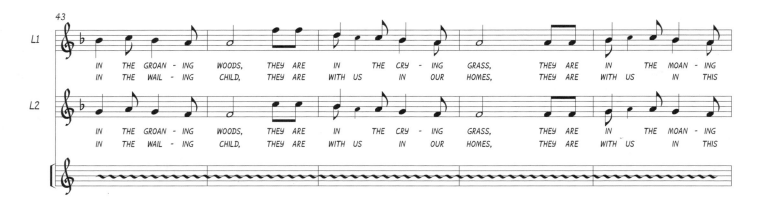

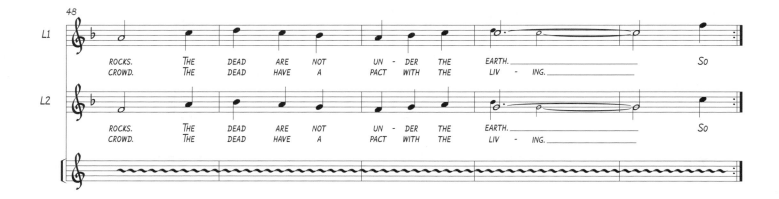

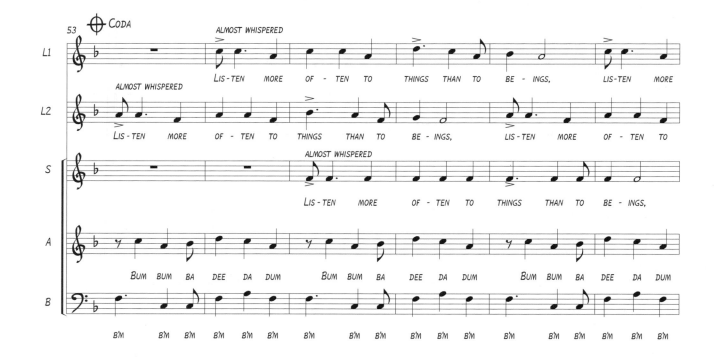

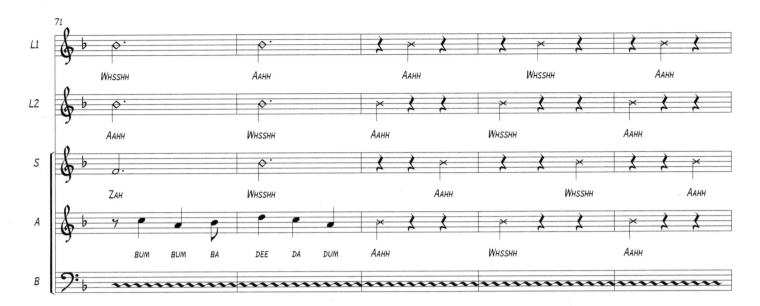

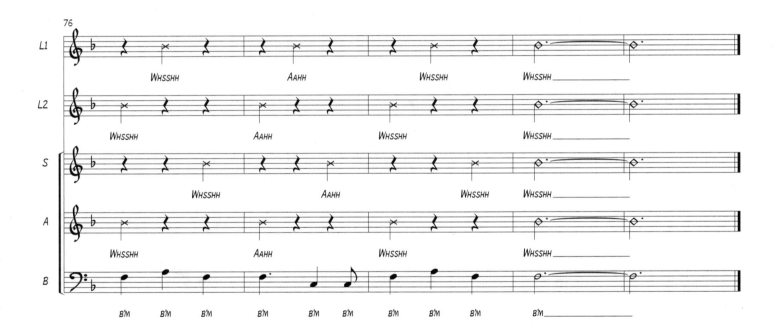

Would You Harbor Me?

FROM *SAFEHOUSE: STILL LOOKING*

WORDS AND MUSIC BY
YSAYE M. BARNWELL

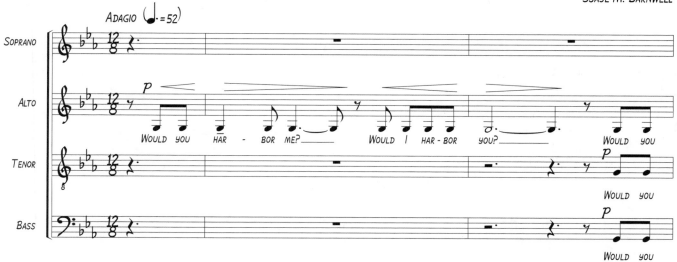

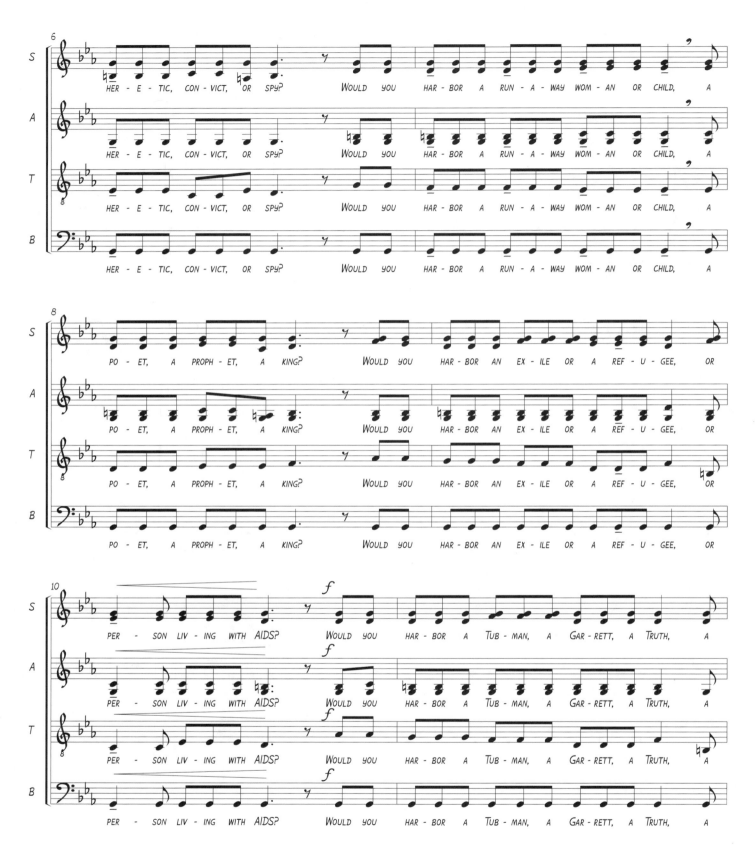

We Are...

FROM THE SONG SUITE "LESSONS"; COMMISSIONED BY REDWOOD CULTURAL WORK FOR
THE NEW SPIRITUALS PROJECT AND THE REDWOOD HOUSE CHOIR, IN ASSOCIATION WITH
MUSE WOMEN'S CHOIR AND THE BOYS CHOIR OF HARLEM.

WORDS AND MUSIC BY
YSAYE M. BARNWELL

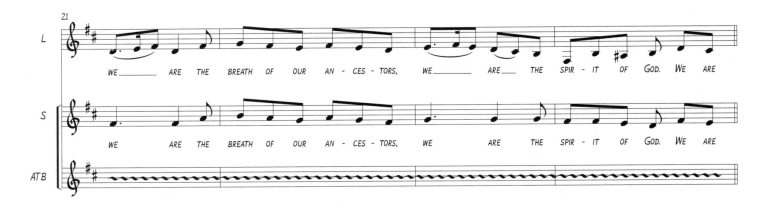

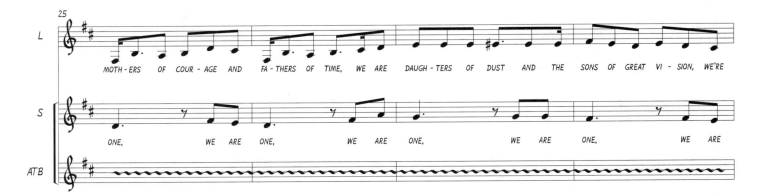

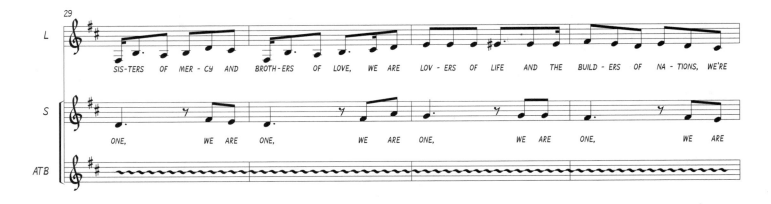

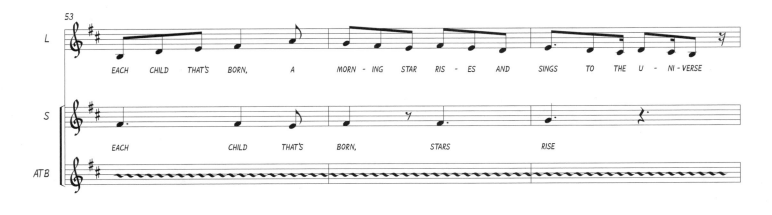

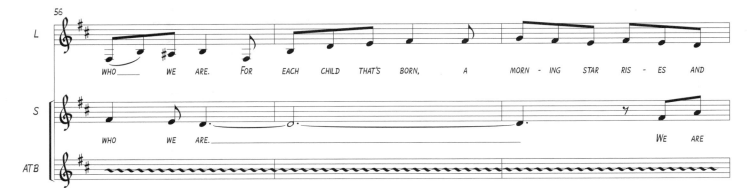

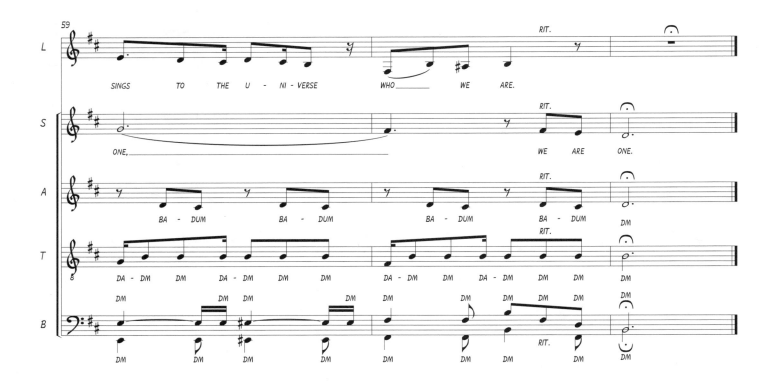

Cum Ba Yah

TRADITIONAL SPIRITUAL
ARR. YSAYE M. BARNWELL

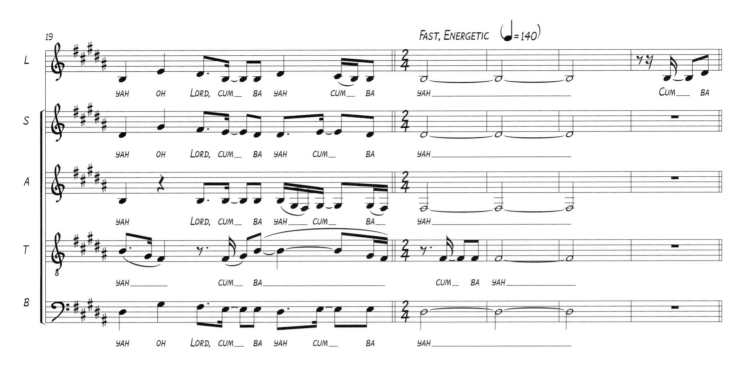

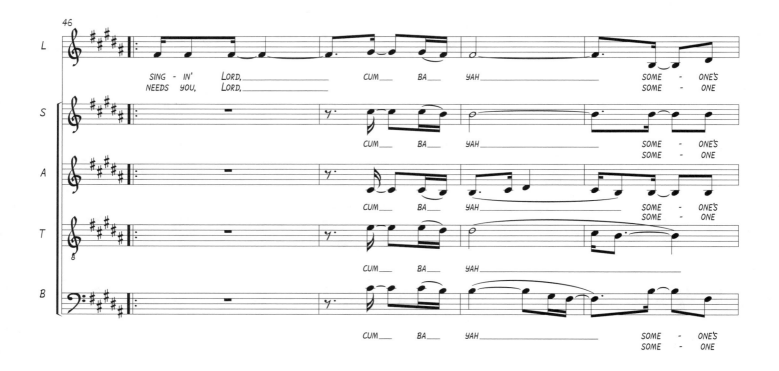

NITANJU BOLADE CASEL
YOUNG AND POSITIVE · INNER VOICES
RUN · DENKO (TRAD./ARR.)

NITANJU BOLADE CASEL, since her return from Africa in 1985, has brought to Sweet Honey In The Rock an ever-unfolding reservoir of traditional African repertoire and jazz, rap and improvisational vocal styles. Her extensive training, research and teaching experience in African-derived traditions has its base in those pioneering communities which led the way in redefining and making accessible African expressive culture in the USA.

While attending Northeastern University in Boston, Massachusetts, as a political science major, she became a professional dancer, teaching at Boston University, Roxbury Community College, Joy of Movement Center and numerous community organizations. Her skills in choreography, voice, percussion instruments and costume design led her to the position of Artistic Director of the Art of Black Dance and Music, as well as Director of Young Afrique, a children's performance company in Lynn, Massachusetts.

Casel came to Sweet Honey after four years of studying, performing and cultural organizing in Dakar, Senegal, where she was co-founder (with Marie Guinier) of ADEA, Artistes des Échanges Africaines. Dedicated to the exchange of ideas and services between Africans of the Diaspora, ADEA worked with local artists, the National Council of Negro Women, The National Theatre Daniel Sorano, the University of Dakar, Air Afrique, the Office of Radio and Television of Senegal (ORTS), the Schomberg Center for Research and Development and the late Dr. Ewart Guinier of Harvard University.

After relocating to Washington, D.C., Casel was awarded a grant from the D.C. Commission of Arts and Humanities to teach dance in the school system. Her compositions are featured in Silver, Burdett & Ginn's World of Music textbook for children, and were heard on the TV pilot of *The Box* by Robert de Niro's Tribeca Production Company. Casel was a guest artist in the Smithsonian Institution's production of *Duke Ellington's Great Ladies of Song*, as well as on the recording of "The Drummer's Path" (Sule Wilson). Currently, she is co-director of First World Productions, a cultural and educational organization in the performance arts. In 1998 she made her debut film appearance in *Beloved*, directed by Jonathan Demme. She is the wife of Mfundishi Tayari Casel and mother of Obadele Jumoke Ajamu JaJa Bayete Casel.

YOUNG AND POSITIVE
LYRICS AND MUSIC BY NITANJU BOLADE CASEL
A Rap Poem

I am young and I am positive
I am the future, I'm gonna tell it like it is
I won't let anything stand in my way
My eyes are on the prize and they will stay that way.

I've got self respect and a whole lot of pride
I won't let you pull me down into a negative stride
Down a dead end street where only trouble lies
That's not the way to keep my eyes on the prize.

This is the nineties and it's a difficult thing
To maintain focus on my visions and dreams
Violence, and abuse of drugs
Turns an innocent child into a vicious thug

Take a close look at this society
At the status of the youth and you will see
A sad situation that is out of hand
Youth are in trouble all over the land.

Don't let this state of affairs bring us down
We have to work together, change things around
I start every day by taking the time
To remind myself, repeat one more time that

I am young and I am positive
I am the future, I'm gonna tell it like it is
I won't let anything stand in my way
My eyes are on the prize and they will stay that way.

I'll teach you, and you teach me
We'll exchange information on how to be
The best we can be, not anything less
It has nothing to do with how we look or dress

It's not material things that make us who we are
Not the sneakers, not the jewelry, not the clothes, or the cars
It's not the job, not the money, nor the status size
That's only momentary pleasure, not a valuable prize

Honesty and truth rank high on my list
Caring and respect for others help to assist me
'Cause I choose to move with love in my heart
For my sisters and my brothers
In every part of the world

You know, it doesn't make sense
To discriminate or believe in hate
Put down another because of their color or race

I must appreciate all the differences of each nationality
I don't want everybody to be like me
Can you imagine everyone exactly the same?
Life would be so boring, I would go insane

I love the fact that each person is unique
The way we think, feel, look and express our needs
So let's move up to a positive tip
Ex racism. It's a negative trip!

Another dead end street
Don't even go down there
Let's accept one another and begin to care
Uplift ourselves, enrich our minds
And every day try to find a little bit of time to say

I am young and I am positive
I am the future, I'm gonna tell it like it is
I won't let anything stand in my way
My eyes are on the prize and they will stay that way.

I don't dis' my elders, they deserve respect
As a matter of fact I do my best to protect
Those who came before me, who struggled and fought
So that I would have a chance to listen up
and be taught

I turn off the TV, I open up a book
I use my imagination and try to be aware as I look
And wonder what the future will be
With pollution destroying the land and the seas,
Nuclear war, greenhouse effect
More toxic waste than ever before

I need all of you adults to live as if you care
Your greedy style of living is my nightmare
I need a world of clean air I can breathe
Where I can drink the water and enjoy the trees
Recycle all your plastic, bottles and glass

I am young and I am positive
I am the future, I'm gonna tell it like it is
I won't let anything stand in my way
My eyes are on the prize and they will stay that way.

Don't leave it up to me to clean up your act
All your oil spills, all the needless deaths
Now you want to leave the planet and
go somewhere else?
To the moon? Or Mars? You had better beware
You'll do the same thing when you get up there

So just don't forget when you turn around
I'll be standing right behind you with a serious frown
'Cause every time I hear an older person say:
"What's wrong with the young folks of today?"

I want to scream
You know what I mean?
Give us support to fulfill our dreams

When I pick up a paper or turn on the news
I'm overwhelmed by the negative views
I would rather hear about the successes of life
Not just the tragedy, not just the strife,
So if nothing else, I must encourage myself
Find a little bit of time to enrich my mind, 'cause

I am young and I am positive
I am the future, I'm gonna tell it like it is
I won't let anything stand in my way
My eyes are on the prize and they will stay that way.

I've got self-respect and a whole lot of pride
I won't let you pull me down into a negative stride
Down a dead end street where only trouble lies
That's not the way to keep my eyes on the prize, 'cause

I am young and I am positive.

INNER VOICES
LYRICS AND MUSIC BY NITANJU BOLADE CASEL

Inner voices...
Inner voices...
Inner voices...
Inner voices...

Listen! Listen!
Listen! Listen!

Listen to these words
I know they are true
Guiding your life
Always helping you...
Listen to these words
A message from your soul
Feel your life change
When your spirit's in control...

Listen! Listen!
Listen! Listen!

I listen to the voice
that speaks to me each day
I open up my mind
and hear what it has to say
This voice is my guide
keeping my life in tune
With the melody of the sun
and the harmony of the moon...

Listen! Listen!
Listen! Listen!

Listening is a quality
not very easy to find
Most folks are so busy talking
that they rarely have the time
To look inside for the answers of life
And that is where they happen to be
We let external things distract us from finding our true
destiny...

Listen! Listen!
Listen! Listen!

How many times have you asked yourself why
You didn't listen to the voice
You let it pass on by
Then you discover you're in trouble
Wondering what went wrong
And you remember that your spirit
Tried to sing this song...
Inner voices...
Inner voices...
Inner voices...
Inner voices...

Listen closely to the voice
that speaks to you each day
Open up your mind and your heart
and try to hear what it has to say
This voice is your guide
in touch with all your inner needs
Connected to your higher consciousness
And the fulfillment of your dreams...

Listen.

RUN

LYRICS AND MUSIC BY NITANJU BOLADE CASEL

No one has the right to hurt me.
Especially when they say they love me
Apologies don't make anything better
So, I'll take my love and my life
And leave today...

Run... to a shelter
Run... to a friend
Run... for my life
Before it comes to an end.

I am gonna run
far away from here
No more cussing, no more fighting
and living in fear.

I am gonna run
far away from you
I have come to my senses
and I don't need you.

I am gonna run
gonna leave you today
'Cause I know there's got to be
a better way.

I am gonna run,
take my children's hands.
We are leaving this nightmare
as fast as we can...

I don't even know
in which direction I should go
But I'm sure it's the right thing to do
It's time to make a move.
The first time I was shoved
I should have been out the door.
But I accepted the apologies
and opened myself up for more...
Abuses
Excuses
Abuses
Excuse me!
I don't have to live this way.
I'm leaving you today.
Abuses
Excuses
Abuses
Excuse me!
I don't have to suffer anymore
I'm walking right out of the door...

Run... to a shelter
Run... to a friend
Run... for my life
Before it comes to an end.

Some of my so-called "friends"
advise me to stick around,
But they're not the ones getting cursed, slapped
or beaten down to the ground.

They say financial security
is hard to come by for a woman like me
And for the children I need a good home
So I should sacrifice until they're grown
Abuses
Excuses
Abuses
Excuse me!

I don't have to suffer anymore
I'm walking right out of that door.
Abuses
Excuses
Abuses
Excuse me!
I don't have to live this way.
I'm leaving you today...

I am gonna run
far away from here
No more cussing, no more fighting
and living in fear.

I am gonna run
far away from you
I have come to my senses
and I don't need you.

I am gonna run
gonna leave you today
'Cause I know there's got to be
a better way.

I am gonna run,
take my children's hands.
We are leaving this nightmare
as fast as we can...

Now, I don't blame myself
for the present situation.
For this kind of behavior
there is no justification

I'm looking ahead to the future
but I won't forget the past
I won't repeat this part of my life
(I'm thankful) it's over at last. No more...
Abuses
Excuses
Abuses
Excuse me!
I don't have to suffer anymore
I'm walking right out that door
Abuses
Excuses
Abuses
Excuse me!
I don't have to live this way
I'm leaving you today...

Run... to a shelter
Run... to a friend
Run... for my life

Before it comes to an end.

I am gonna run
far away from here
No more cussing, no more fighting
and living in fear.

I am gonna run
far away from you
I have come to my senses
and I don't need you
I am gonna run
gonna leave you today.
'Cause I know there's got to be
a better way

I am gonna run,
take my children's hands.
We are leaving this nightmare
as fast as we can...

Run... mmmm
Run... mmmm
Run!!!

DENKO

TRAD. BAMBARA SONG FROM MALI
ARR. BY NITANJU BOLADE CASEL

Denko et denko ye
Mousoo lou ye ne na koun ye
Denko ye
Tieba i kan son dola

Teiba y ma na sa domina
Tieba koro doun ka sa nou fa
Ka son be mon nyenema

Teiba y ma na sa domina
Tieba koro doun ka sa nou fa
Mine be mou ye ne maa

COMPOSER'S NOTES

YOUNG AND POSITIVE

Composed in the rap tradition, "Young and Positive" was created out of a need I had to offer positive encouragement and affirmation to young people, to give them something they could sing on a regular basis that would hopefully help them feel uplifted and inspired. It is a reminder that in spite of all the negative things going on in the world, there are still ways that they control that will allow them to rise to another level. This song can be for all voices, although it is probably best for the voices of young people. Instruments can be used to create a larger sound, and improvisation is encouraged — especially in the phrasing of the lyrics within the rhythms.

INNER VOICES

My own inner voice led me to write "Inner Voices," dictating its own rhythm and blues flavor. A lifetime of experiences in which I found myself either delightfully pleased that I had listened, or painfully aware that I had not listened to my inner voice (inner God, inner Goodness, Inner G, energy!), has created a profound respect and love for the wisdom that lies within the silence of my soul.

This song is for all voices and has a lead/backup arrangement. Instruments would create a larger sound and improvisation is encouraged, especially in the lead phrasing around the melody. The tempo can slow down a little. Speeding it up may result in a loss of clarity of the lyrics, particularly in the bridge, which must be articulated by all voices.

RUN!

My first introduction to an abusive relationship occurred years ago when a friend knocked on my door wanting a place to stay. I opened my home for her safety and that is probably when this song began. Since that time I have watched countless interviews of the abused as well as abusers, apathy among law officials, stalkings and murders, all of which have left me with a queasy nervousness and raging anger that this could happen. How could they stay? I would ask myself over and over again. I had never been in this kind of relationship with a man so my frame of reference was very narrow. But as time went by, I really tried to listen to what these victims were saying, and I began to understand... "Run!"

"Run!" has a rhythm and blues feel and is for all voices. A few instruments would enhance the sound, but add too many and things will start to sound cluttered. The rhythm should remind one of the breaths that come from running, and the pulse should be a heartbeat (luba duba) full of fear and conviction.

DENKO

"Denko" is a song from Mali, West Africa and is sung in the Bambara language. "Denko" means to have a child. The song talks about a woman who wants to conceive and about the prayers offered to bring forth this new life. Once the new life has arrived, however, there is a realization that the prayers must not only continue but intensify in order for this child to thrive.

I learned this song during my first trip to West Africa in 1979, after a long, grueling trip from Dakar, Senegal to Bamako, Mali on a train called the Bamako Express (which somehow didn't quite feel like an express during the more than 30-hour experience). It was well worth the journey; during my time there, one of the women shared this song with me. I had no idea then how deeply it would affect my life personally.

In this arrangement, the opening call is sung in its traditional form as I learned it, with the addition of the choral response. The rhythm is free-form. I have arranged the second, up-tempo, section for lead voice, chorus and bass voice. The use of percussion instruments is highly recommended and the rhythm of the instruments should become a driving force.

The vocal placement for this song is frontal/nasal, which is typical and indicative of the region of its origin.

Young and Positive

Words and Music by
Nitanju Bolade Casel

NINE - TIES AND IT'S A DIF - FI - CULT THING____ TO MAIN - TAIN FO - CUS ON MY VI - SIONS AND DREAMS____

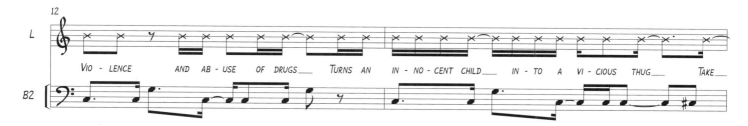

VIO - LENCE AND AB - USE OF DRUGS____ TURNS AN IN - NO - CENT CHILD____ IN - TO A VI - CIOUS THUG____ TAKE____

____ A CLOSE LOOK AT THIS SO - CI - E - TY____ AT THE STA - TUS OF THE YOUTH AND YOU____ WILL SEE____ A

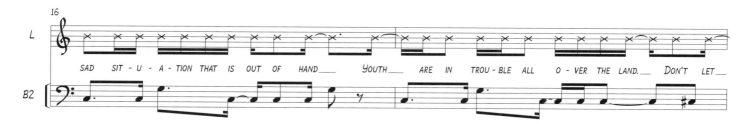

SAD SIT - U - A - TION THAT IS OUT OF HAND____ YOUTH____ ARE IN TROU - BLE ALL O - VER THE LAND.____ DON'T LET____

____ THIS STATE OF AF - FAIRS BRING US DOWN____ WE HAVE TO WORK TO - GETH - ER, CHANGE THINGS A - ROUND____ I

START EV - 'RY DAY BY TAK - ING THE TIME____ TO RE - MIND MY - SELF, RE - PEAT ONE MORE TIME THAT I AM

JOB, NOT THE MON - EY, NOR THE STA - TUS SIZE___ THAT'S ON - LY MO - MEN - TAR - Y PLEA - SURE, NOT A VAL - UA - BLE PRIZE___

HON - ES - TY AND TRUTH RANK HIGH___ ON MY LIST CAR - ING AND RE - SPECT FOR OTH - ERS HELP TO AS - SIST___ ME 'CAUSE I

CHOOSE TO MOVE___ WITH LOVE___ IN MY HEART FOR MY SIS - TERS AND MY BROTH - ERS IN EV - ER - Y PART___ OF THE

WORLD YOU KNOW, IT DOES - N'T MAKE SENSE TO DIS - CRIM - I - NATE___ OR BE - LIEVE IN HATE PUT___

___ DOWN AN - OTH - ER BE - CAUSE___ OF THEIR COL - OR OR RACE I MUST AP - PRE - CI - ATE___ ALL THE

DIFF-'REN-CES OF EACH NA-TION-AL-I-TY___ I DON'T WANT EV-'RY-BOD-Y TO BE___ LIKE ME___ CAN YOU IM-

AG-INE EV-'RY-ONE EX-ACT-LY THE SAME?___ LIFE WOULD BE SO BOR-ING I WOULD GO IN-SANE___ I

LOVE THE FACT THAT EACH PER-SON IS U-NIQUE___ THE WAY WE THINK, FEEL, LOOK, AND EX-PRESS OUR NEEDS___ SO

LET'S MOVE UP TO A POS-I-TIVE TIP___ EX RAC-IS-M. IT'S A NEG-A-TIVE TRIP!___ AN-OTH-ER

DEAD-END STREET___ DON'T E-VEN GO DOWN THERE___ LET'S AC-CEPT ONE AN-OTH-ER AND BE-GIN TO CARE___ UP-

LIFT OUR - SELVES,___ EN - RICH OUR MINDS___ AND EV - 'RY DAY TRY TO FIND A LIT - TLE BIT OF TIME TO SAY I'M

LEAD ALONE:

___ ARE ON THE PRIZE AND THEY WILL STAY THAT WAY. I DON'T DIS' MY ELD - ERS, THEY DE - SERVE RE - SPECT As A

YOUNG AND POS - I - TIVE___ BA DA M BA DA BI DI BA DA M BA DA BI DI

YOUNG AND POS - I - TIVE___ BI BI DY BA BI BI DY BA BI BI DY BA

YOUNG AND POS - I - TIVE___ BI DI BA DA BA DA BI DI BA DA BA DA

DOON DA DOON DOON___ DOON DA DOON

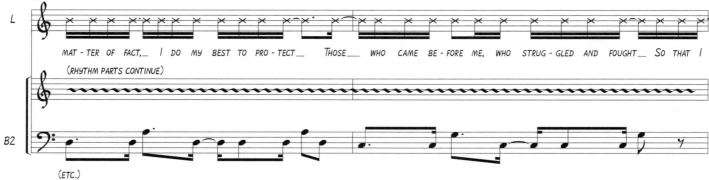

MAT - TER OF FACT,___ I DO MY BEST TO PRO - TECT___ THOSE___ WHO CAME BE - FORE ME, WHO STRUG - GLED AND FOUGHT___ SO THAT I

(RHYTHM PARTS CONTINUE)

(ETC.)

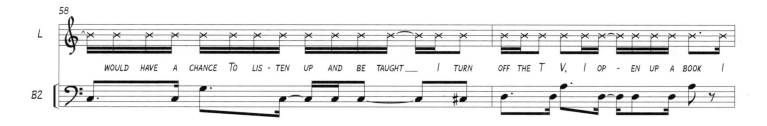

WOULD HAVE A CHANCE TO LIS-TEN UP AND BE TAUGHT___ I TURN OFF THE T V, I OP-EN UP A BOOK I

USE MY I-MAG-I-NA-TION AND TRY___ TO BE A-WARE AS I LOOK AND WON-DER WHAT THE FU-TURE WILL BE___ WITH POL-

LU - TION DE-STROY-ING THE LAND___ AND THE SEAS, NU-CLE-AR WAR, GREEN-HOUSE EF-FECT___ MORE

TOX - IC WASTE___ THAN EV-ER BE-FORE___ I NEED ALL OF YOU AD-ULTS TO LIVE AS IF YOU CARE___ YOUR

GREED - Y STYLE OF LIV-ING IS MY___ NIGHT-MARE___ I NEED A WORLD OF CLEAN AIR I CAN BREATHE___ WHERE

I CAN DRINK THE WA-TER AND EN-JOY THE TREES___ RE - CY-CLE ALL YOUR PLAS - TIC, BOT-TLES AND GLASS___ DON'T LEAVE___

D.S.

IT UP TO ME TO CLEAN UP YOUR ACT_____ 'CAUSE I AM

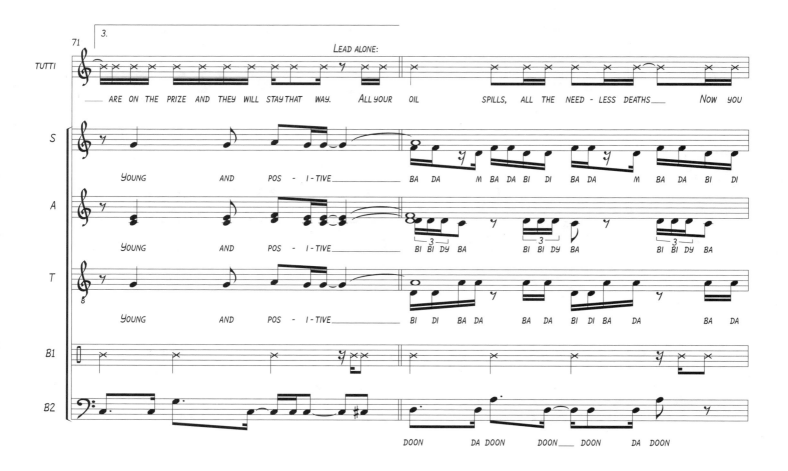

3.

Lead alone:

___ ARE ON THE PRIZE AND THEY WILL STAY THAT WAY. ALL YOUR OIL SPILLS, ALL THE NEED - LESS DEATHS___ Now YOU

YOUNG AND POS - I - TIVE_____ BA DA M BA DA BI DI BA DA M BA DA BI DI

YOUNG AND POS - I - TIVE_____ BI BI DY BA BI BI DY BA BI BI DY BA

YOUNG AND POS - I - TIVE_____ BI DI BA DA BA DA BI DI BA DA BA DA

DOON DA DOON DOON___ DOON DA DOON

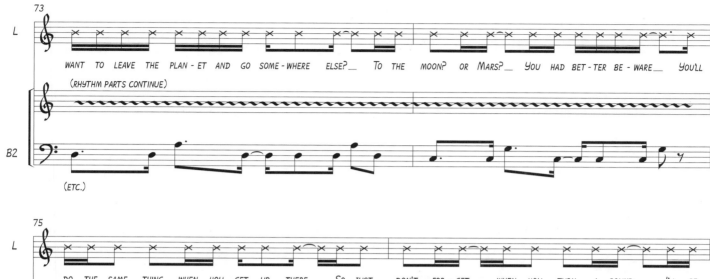

WANT TO LEAVE THE PLAN - ET AND GO SOME - WHERE ELSE?__ TO THE MOON? OR MARS? YOU HAD BET - TER BE - WARE__ YOU'LL

(RHYTHM PARTS CONTINUE)

(ETC.)

DO THE SAME THING WHEN YOU GET UP THERE__ SO JUST DON'T FOR - GET__ WHEN YOU TURN A - ROUND__ I'LL BE

STAND - ING RIGHT BE - HIND YOU WITH A SE - RI - OUS FROWN__ 'CAUSE EV - 'RY TIME I HEAR AN OLD - ER PER - SON SAY:__

SOLO VOICE:

"WHAT'S

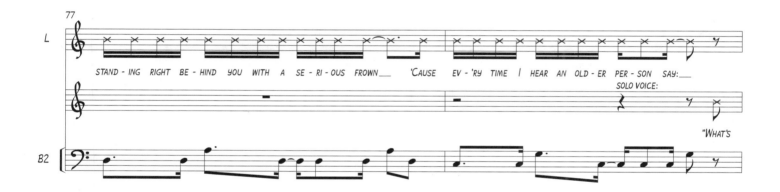

I WANT TO SCREAM YOU KNOW WHAT I MEAN?__ GIVE US SUP -

WRONG WITH THE YOUNG FOLKS OF TO - DAY?"__

TUTTI:

AH!_____

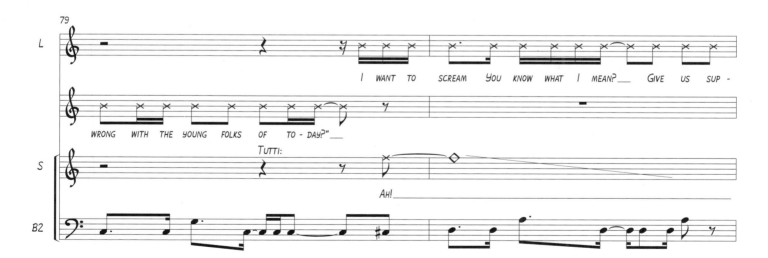

PORT TO FUL-FILL OUR DREAMS___ WHEN I PICK UP A PA-PER OR TURN___ ON THE NEWS I'M O-VER-

WHELMED BY THE NEG-A-TIVE VIEWS___ I WOULD RATH-ER HEAR A-BOUT THE SUC-CESS-ES OF LIFE___ NOT JUST THE

TRAG-E-DY, NOT___ JUST THE STRIFE, SO IF NO-THING ELSE,___ I MUST EN-COUR-AGE MY-SELF___ FIND A

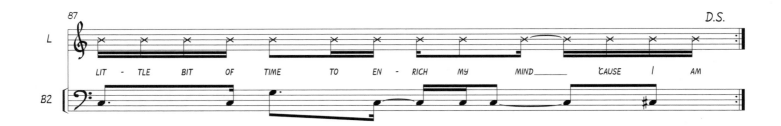

LIT-TLE BIT OF TIME TO EN-RICH MY MIND___ 'CAUSE I AM

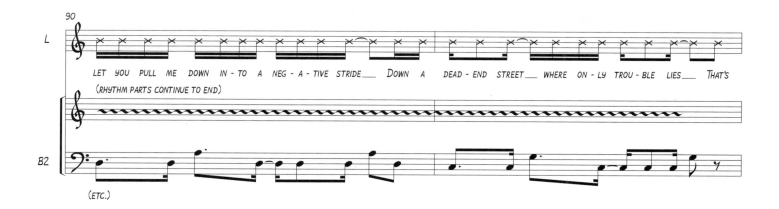

INNER VOICES

WORDS AND MUSIC BY
NITANJU BOLADE CASEL

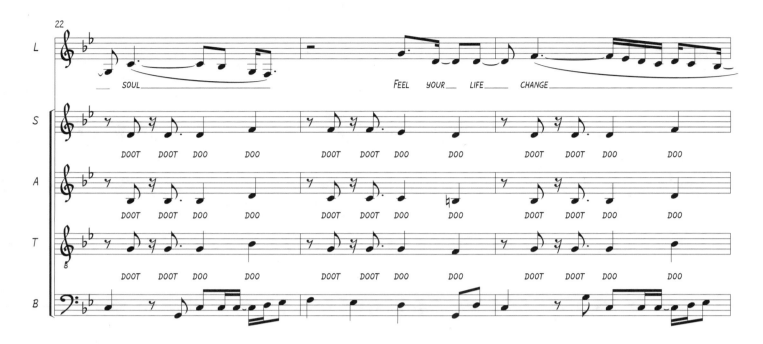

4TH TIME TO CODA ⊕

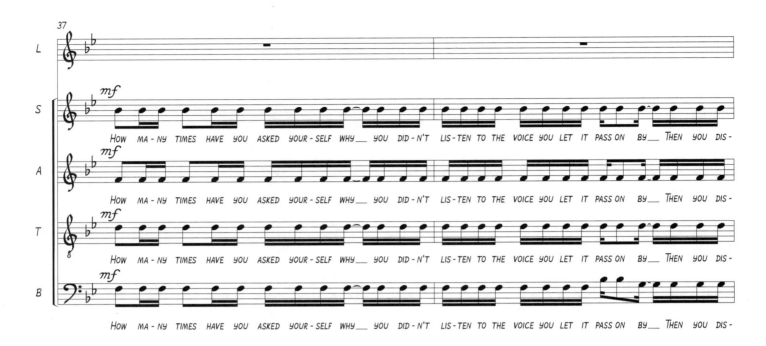

*REFER TO THE RECORDING FOR ACCURATE PERFORMANCE OF LEAD LINE

2. I LISTEN TO THE VOICE THAT SPEAKS TO ME EACH DAY
   I OPEN UP MY MIND AND HEAR WHAT IT HAS TO SAY
   THIS VOICE IS MY GUIDE KEEPING MY LIFE IN TUNE
   WITH THE MELODY OF THE SUN AND THE HARMONY OF THE MOON.

3. LISTENING IS A QUALITY NOT VERY EASY TO FIND
   MOST FOLKS ARE SO BUSY TALKING THAT THEY RARELY HAVE THE TIME
   TO LOOK INSIDE FOR THE ANSWERS OF LIFE AND THAT IS WHERE THEY HAPPEN TO BE
   WE LET EXTERNAL THINGS DISTRACT US FROM FINDING OUR TRUE DESTINY.

4. LISTEN CLOSELY TO THE VOICE THAT SPEAKS TO YOU EACH DAY
   OPEN UP YOUR MIND AND YOUR HEART AND TRY TO HEAR WHAT IT HAS TO SAY
   THIS VOICE IS YOUR GUIDE IN TOUCH WITH ALL YOUR INNER NEEDS
   CONNECTED TO YOUR HIGHER CONSCIOUSNESS AND THE FULFILLMENT OF YOUR DREAMS.

Run

Words and Music by
Nitanju Bolade Casel

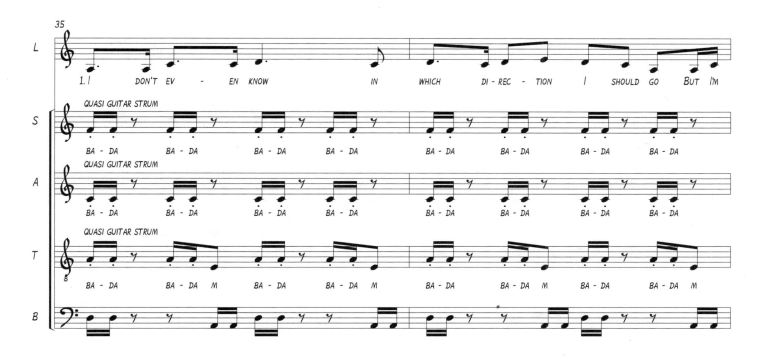

KNOW___ THERE'S___ GOT TO BE A BET-TER WAY.___ I___ AM GON-NA RUN,___ TAKE MY CHILD-REN'S HANDS___

WE ARE LEAV-ING THIS NIGHT-MARE AS FAST AS WE___ CAN___

RUN TO A SHEL - TER RUN TO A FRIEND___ RUN FOR MY LIFE BE-FORE IT

[IMPROV. FOR 16 BARS ON PHRASES "RUN TO A SHELTER," "RUN TO A FRIEND," "SAVE YOUR LIFE," "BEFORE IT ENDS"]

3. Now, I don't blame myself
for the present situation
For this kind of behavior
there is no justification

I'm looking ahead to the future
but I won't forget the past
I won't repeat this part of my life
(I'm thankful) it's over at last. No more...

Denko

TRADITIONAL BAMBARA
ARRANGED BY NITANJU BOLADE CASEL

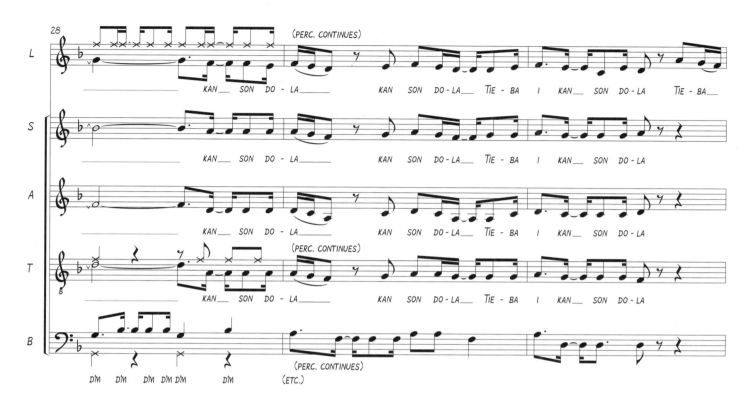

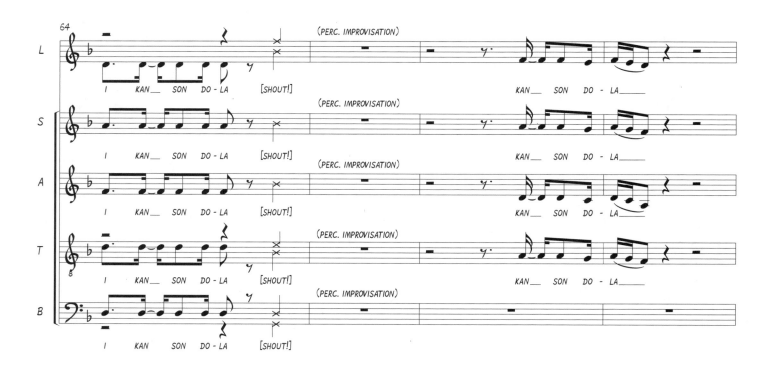

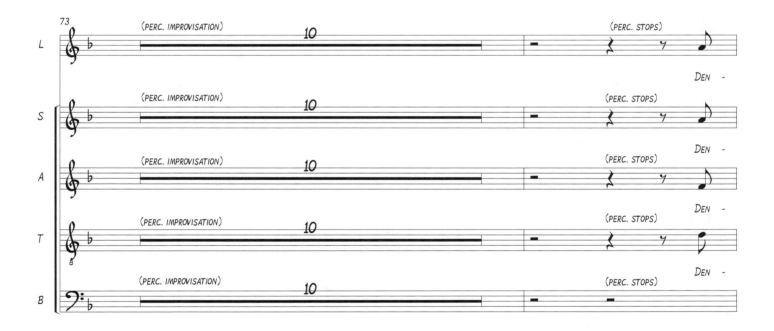

AISHA KAHLIL
DREAM SONGS OF LOVE · FULANI CHANT
WODAABE NIGHTS · ALUNDE (TRAD./ARR.)

AISHA KAHLIL joined Sweet Honey In The Rock in 1981. An experienced singer of jazz and of African song and dance performance traditions, she moved the ensemble into new ground in its exploration of vocal improvisation. She is Sweet Honey In The Rock's strongest blues singer, a genre she had not previously explored before coming to the group. Some of the group's most innovative and experimental work occurs in the performance of her compositions, including "Fulani Chant" and "Wodaabe Nights."

In 1993, Kahlil was named Best Professional Soloist in the Contemporary A Cappella Recording Awards for her performances of "See See Rider" and "Fulani Chant" on Sweet Honey In The Rock's recording *In This Land* (EarthBeat! Records).

In her work as a performing artist and master teacher in voice and dance, Kahlil specializes in the integration of traditional and contemporary forms of music, dance and theater. She has performed as a vocalist and dancer with the Raymond Sawyer Dance Theater, Halifu Osumare, The Sounds of Awareness, Sundance and the African Heritage Dancers and Drummers. In 1980, she created the musical *2000 Seasons - From Nile to Now* with Anedra Shockley and Talib Kibwe, and performed it in various venues throughout New York City and at the D.C. Black Repertory Theater. Ms. Kahlil has performed off Broadway at the Public Theater in Liz Swaddo's production of *The Haggaddah*.

In 1981, she founded the First World Dance Theater and is co-director with Nitanju Bolade Casel of First World Productions. For 10 years she served on the faculty of the Levine School of Music in Washington, D.C., as Artistic Director of the Outreach Dance Ensemble and The Levine Dancers and Drummers. She has taught and lectured at the University of Hawaii at Manoa and has performed as special guest artist for the Lanaii Artist Series with her ensemble Aisha Kahlil and Friends.

Ms. Kahlil has taught at the Institute for Contemporary Dance, Leslie College, The Joy of Movement, Dance Works, Dance Place and the D.C. Black Repertory Theater. She is currently on the faculty of the New Sewell Music School in Washington, D.C.

A debut film appearance in *Beloved*, directed by Jonathan Demme, has recently been added to her acting credits. To her film score credits can be added "Fulani Chant," from the soundtrack of the film *Down In The Delta*, directed by Maya Angelou. "Mandiacapella" and "Wodaabe Nights" appear on the soundtrack of *Africans in America*, a film series produced by WGBH Boston for PBS.

FULANI CHANT
MUSIC BY AISHA KAHLIL

A tone poem without words.

DREAM SONGS OF LOVE
LYRICS AND MUSIC BY AISHA KAHLIL

Dreams of love flow through the air,
Bright magic, love's magic is everywhere

A soothing thought, a healing prayer,
Love's beauty, God's beauty beyond compare

Dream songs of beauty
True beauty that flows from within

Love's healing magic
Filling our hearts once again, forever.

WODAABE NIGHTS
MUSIC BY AISHA KAHLIL

A tone poem without words.

ALUNDE
TRAD./ARR. BY AISHA KAHLIL
(phonetic spelling)

Ah - lun - day	Ah - lun - day	(AYE)
Ah - lun - day	Ah - loo - yah	(AYE)
Ah - lun - day	Ah - lun - day	(AYE)
Ah - lun - day	Ah - loo - yah	(AYE)

Ah - jah - bo Ah - jay - bo
Ah - nay coo - po - o
Ai yai yeh
Ah - lun - day
Ah - lun - day

COMPOSER'S NOTES

FULANI CHANT

"Fulani Chant" was composed at the end of a long rehearsal session during which Nitanju Bolade Casel and I were preparing for the premier performance of our music and dance ensemble, Fulani! After everyone had gone home, I went into prayerful meditation while listening to the song of those birds that herald the end of night and the beginning of dawn, and the strains of this melody came to me – a haunting melody accentuated by the percussive, rhythmic cacophony of those winged servants of Allah. At the rehearsal session the next evening, I taught it to the ensemble and it was performed as the opening number in the concert. I later taught this piece to Sweet Honey and a progressive evolution of the improvisation began to unfold with each performance. "Fulani Chant" works well with a small ensemble or a large choir. The principal soloist should state the opening theme of the melody and begin developing the improvisation section, but can be joined after a point by one or several vocalists. The rhythmic background should be maintained throughout the composition. The lower voice(s) should approximate the sound and quality of the talking drum.

DREAM SONGS OF LOVE

This song speaks to the power of our own dreams: our thoughts, our vision to achieve and effect healing change in ourselves and in the lives of those around us. It has a light, airy, dreamy quality, and is written in the jazz mode. If performed by a small ensemble, the members should think of their voices as instruments in a small jazz ensemble. The percussion part should have a light quality, with the voice sliding up for each note to simulate a cross between an acoustic bass and a talking drum. The improvised section can be done as a solo, duet or by a group, but should maintain a tranquil, meditative quality. During the improvised section, the percussion part should also free up and become more accentuated.

WODAABE NIGHTS

The Wodaabe are a nomadic tribe of people in Sub-Saharan Africa who are related to the larger group of Fulani. While the Fulani were among the first to embrace Islam, setting up stationary households and intermingling with other ethnic groups, the Wodaabe maintained their traditional culture and nomadic lifestyle. As my own African ancestral origins reach back to the Fulani, I feel closely connected in two deep ways to the roots of these people.

In this "Wodaabe Nights," which is in no way traditional, I have tried to imagine some of the musical offerings that might spring forth on a typical evening in the ancient world of the Fulani people.

The solo line in this composition is largely improvised while the rhythmic lines are cyclical, repetitive and should be performed with precision. A number of instruments – e.g., rattles, shakers, rain sticks, drum-head tambourines – can be used to enhance the feeling in the piece.

ALUNDE

"Alunde" was taught to me as a young child by the late, great Pearl Primus, who visited our school with her large entourage. Ms. Primus taught us this song as a lullaby, but I don't recall that she told us the country of origin, the language it was sung in or the specific translation of the lyrics that were taught in the oral tradition. The lyrics in the transcription are presented as a phonetic representation of what I learned.

Alunde lends itself well to a large group, but is also effective in a smaller ensemble. Take care to implement a touch of nasality in the vocal timbre, but lush vibrato also works well with this beautiful melody. The ending phrase, lun-day, should be repeated and grooved upon in a complex vocal improvisation which is done by the entire ensemble. This ending section should involve a cacophony of calls, shouts, harmonic lines, etc. It should almost lose the rhythmic structure, which is maintained subtly underneath and is then reinstated at the end of the arrangement.

Recent inquiries have led to a song written and recorded by Babatunde Olatunji called Odun De. He states that his song is based on a traditional Yoruba thanks-giving chant celebrating the harvest and new year. Clearly, both melodies are derived from the same root and his transcribed lyrics are as follows:

O-dun de o-dun de

O-dun de a tun yo

O-dun de o-dun de

O-dun de mo tun yo

E dun-ma-re jo-wo wa gbo-pe mi o

I-re i-re———-e————e————-

O-dun de, o-dun de, o-dun de

I-re i-re———-e————e————-

Olatunji- Drums of Passion Songbook

(Reprinted by permission)

Fulani Chant

Aisha Kahlil

[44 BARS IMPROV ON MM. 17-46; RESOLVE ON C]

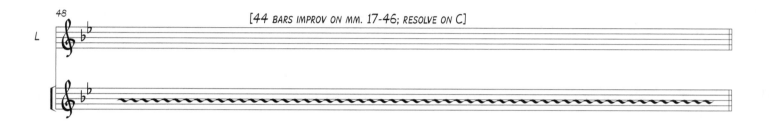

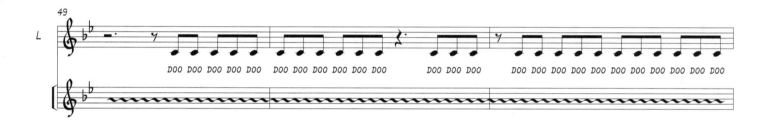

DOO DOO DOO DOO DOO   DOO DOO DOO DOO DOO DOO   DOO DOO DOO   DOO DOO DOO DOO DOO DOO DOO DOO DOO DOO DOO

DOO DOO DOO DOO DOO   (ETC.)

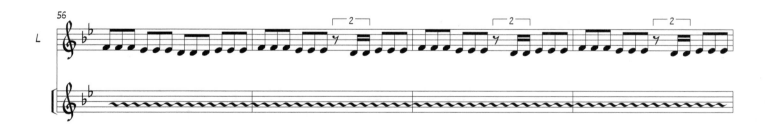

[*44 BARS IMPROV. ON MM. 51-63*]

*Oo*_____

[*44 BARS IMPROV. ON MM. 65-78*]

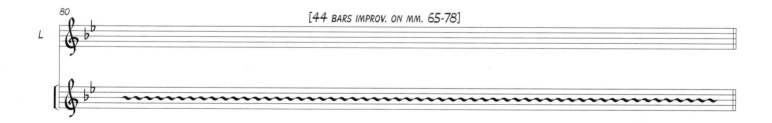

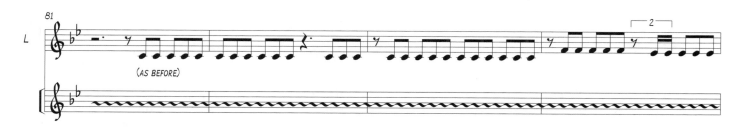

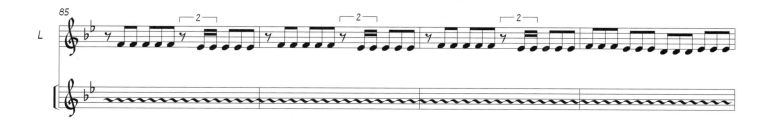

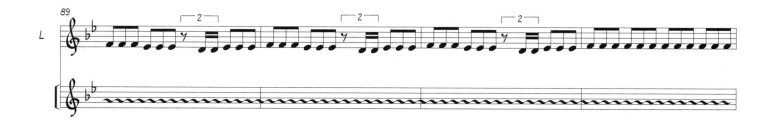

Dream Songs of Love

Words and Muisc by
Aisha Kahlil

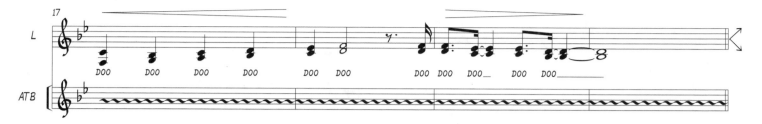

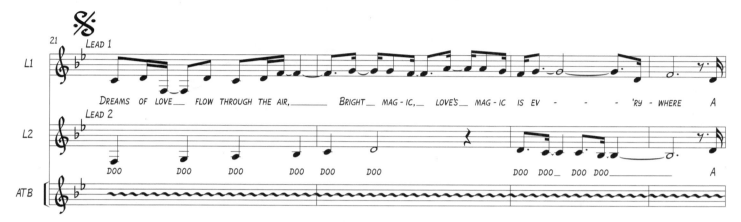

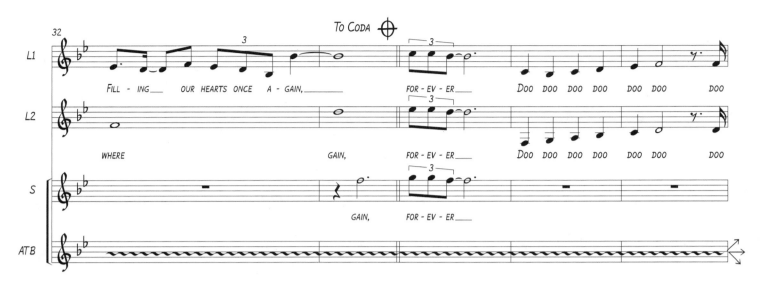

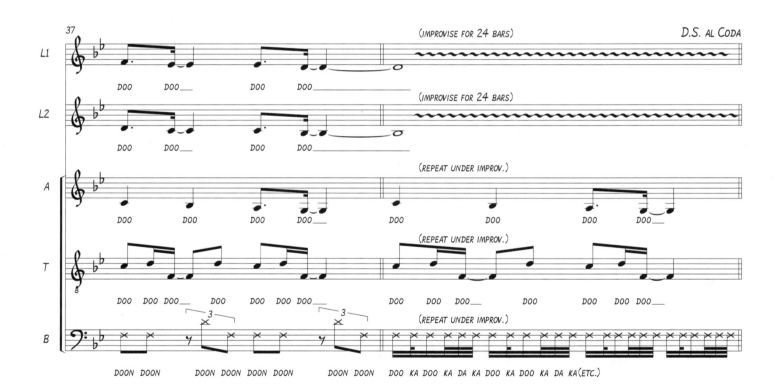

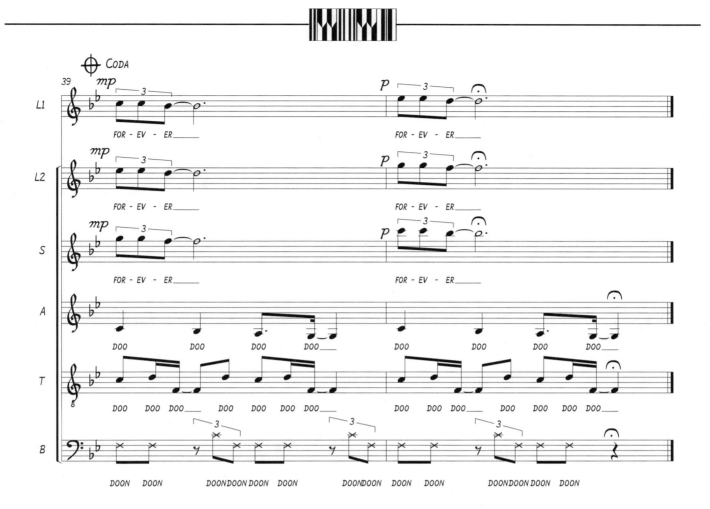

Wodaabe Nights

Aisha Kahlil

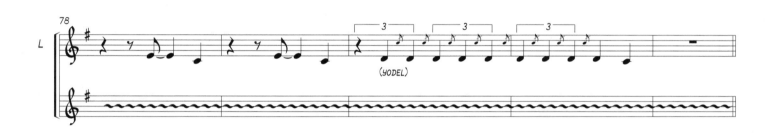

[LEAD IMPROVISES ON THESE FIGURES UNTIL A COMPLETE STATEMENT HAS BEEN MADE, THEN PIECE CONTINUES TO MEASURE 84]

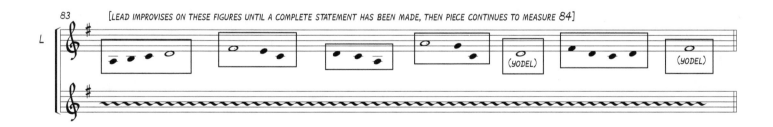

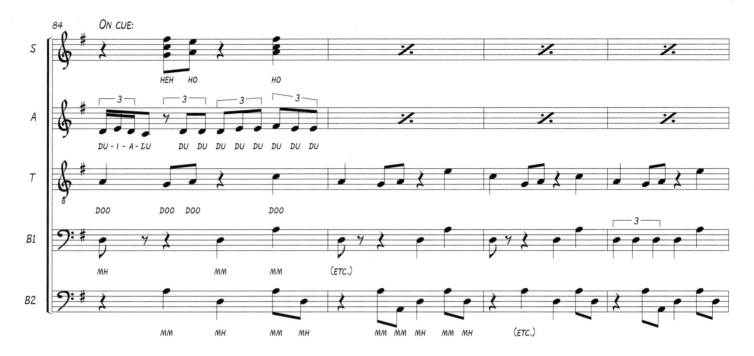

Alunde

TRADITIONAL
ARR. AISHA KAHLIL

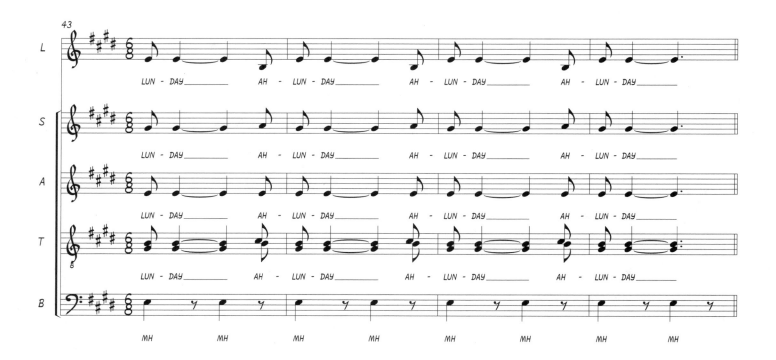

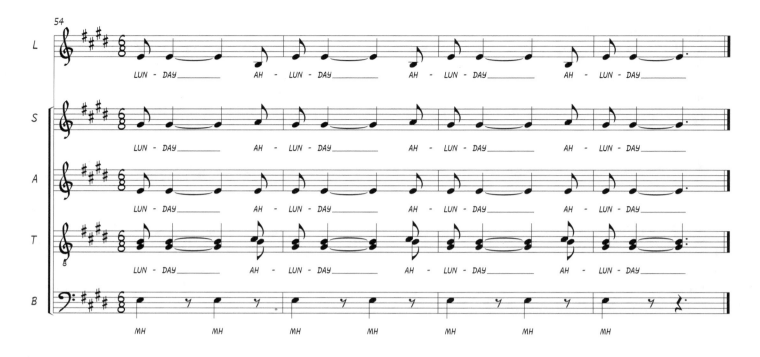

CAROL MAILLARD

STAY · PRAYER TO THE ONE
GOIN' TO SEE MY BABY · MOTHERLESS CHIL' (TRAD./ARR.)

CAROL LYNN MAILLARD was born in North Philadelphia, Pennsylvania, and lived there until leaving for Catholic University (in Washington, D.C.) to major in Violin Performance. Music was always very important to her as a means of self-expression. However, her dream was to become a movie actress even though there were not many Black actresses to watch and enjoy. Catholic University's Drama Department offered many opportunities to discover and explore her talents as an actress, singer and composer. She switched majors and joined the theater program. When the call went out in Washington, D.C. for an open audition to participate in a new professional acting company for African-Americans, she jumped at the chance to realize her dream and auditioned for actor Robert Hooks. Because of the innovative and exciting training the actors received at The D.C. Black Repertory Company in improvisation, scene study, dance, voice and production, Carol was well prepared to be called a triple threat of an artist. Sweet Honey In The Rock, of which she was a founding member, was born out of the vocal workshops conducted at The Rep.

Leaving D.C. to pursue her acting career in New York proved to be a good move and Carol immediately began working in theater, commercials and cabaret. Off Broadway, she worked with many fine directors and playwrights at the New York Shakespeare Festival's Public Theater (*Betsy Brown*, *Spunk*, *Caucasian Chalk Circle*, *A Photograph...*, *Under Fire*) and the Negro Ensemble Company (*The Great MacDaddy*, *Home*, *Colored Peoples' Time*). She also worked at the Actors' Studio, The Amas Repertory Theater, The San Diego Rep and numerous regional theaters and tours. On Broadway, Carol was featured in *Home*, *Comin' Uptown*, *Don't Get God Started*, *Eubie*, *Beehive* and *It's So Nice To Be Civilized*. *For Colored Girls Who Have Considered Suicide...* took her on tour to Australia, then to Los Angeles, then to the premiere season of American Playhouse on PBS, directed by Oz Scott. In 1993, she was featured in the American Playhouse production of *Hallelujah* directed by Charles Lane. Carol also appears in the film *Beloved*, directed by Jonathan Demme.

As a singer, Carol has performed and recorded with Horace Silver (*Music of the Spheres*, Blue Note Records) and Betty Buckley (*An Evening With Betty Buckley at Carnegie Hall*, Sterling Records). She has arranged vocals, been vocal captain, vocal director and has conducted singing ensembles.

New York City is home for Carol and her 12-year old son. Jordan is a violinist and a fantastic basketball player. He gets to perform quite a bit and that is so beautiful to see. Passing music and creativity on to him gives Carol a great sense of wonder and gratitude. Her prayer is that the talents she manages to offer to the universe touch many hearts and encourage them to express themselves fully and with joy.

STAY

LYRICS AND MUSIC BY CAROL MAILLARD

The clock on the wall says it's time to go,
But I know, my heart
Really wants you to stay a while.
Hear the seconds ticking by,
And the world outside is still,
So before you have to leave
Stay a while with me.

Soft breezes, blowing through the air
Summer moon is riding high in the sky
Waves of love are dancing 'round - everywhere
Like golden fireflies in the cool black night
Sittin' here with you is so sweet, so divine
Like the song of the wind,
Whistlin' through the trees,
When I'm with you, babe,
Not a word needs to be said,
Tender love, I'm asking you to
Stay a little bit longer with me.

One light, one breath, one spirit, one heart
One love lives between us
When you drink, my thirst is satisfied
And when I tire, I know
you'll be there to give me rest
Just to live my life with you
would be so sweet, so divine
Like sounds of the wind
whistlin' through the trees
Ancestor rhythms, the sound of two hearts
Dancing love's dance together
Time is movin' on, but I'm asking you to
Stay a little bit longer with me.

PRAYER TO THE ONE
LYRICS AND MUSIC BY CAROL MAILLARD

Sunshine
Or rain
They are
The same
God's love
Love's light
In day
Or night
Why should
I care
If here
Or there
You are
With me
In all
I see
My every breath
My very breath,　You

Glory,
Be Thine
All space
Divine
Spirit
Moves free
From you
Heals me
Why should
I care
If here
Or there
Inside
Holy Light
No day
Or night
My every breath
My very breath,　You

Mother,
Father God
Your home
My heart
My heart
Where you are
So near
Never far
Why should
I care
If here
Or there
You are
With me
In all
I see

Why should
I care
If here
Or there
Ever
With me
In all
I see
My every breath
My very breath,　You

GOIN' TO SEE MY BABY
LYRICS AND MUSIC BY CAROL MAILLARD

VERSE 1
I don't care how I get there but
I got to make this journey - uh huh
He called my name out loud
and Lord knows, I heard him - all right
So I'm packin' up my bags
gon' leave my worries on the doorstep - a big load
'Cause where ever he is,
I'll be right by his side

CHORUS
Hey, I'm goin', goin' to see, see my
Goin' to see my baby,
Goin' to see him right now,
Goin' to see my baby,
Goin' to see him right now.

VERSE 2
It's been years since I've seen him, but my
love gets stronger and stronger - uh huh
Gonna keep on movin'
with my eye on the north star shinin' - all right
So I'm sayin' good-bye to these
four cold walls that surround me - a-real cold
'Cause wherever he is,
I'll be right by his side.

CHORUS
Hey, I'm goin', goin' to see, see my
Goin' to see my baby,
Goin' to see him right now,
Goin' to see my baby,
Goin' to see him right now.

VERSE 3
I don't care how I get there but
I got to make this journey - uh huh
Gonna keep on movin'
with my eye on the north star shinin' - all right
So I'm sayin' good-bye to these
four cold walls that surround me - a-real cold
Hey, 'cause a life all alone
ain't even worth the ride.

CHORUS
Hey, I'm goin', goin' to see, see my
Goin' to see my baby,
Goin' to see him right now...
Goin' to see my baby,
Goin' to see him right now...

MOTHERLESS CHIL'

TRAD. SPIRITUAL / ARR. CAROL MAILLARD

Hmmmm, hmmmm
Sometimes I feel like a motherless chil'
sometimes I feel
sometimes I feel like
sometimes I feel like a motherless chil'
Sometimes I feel like a motherless chil'
sometimes I feel
sometimes I feel like
sometimes I feel like a motherless chil'
Sometimes I feel like a motherless chil'
sometimes I feel
sometimes I feel like
sometimes I feel like a motherless chil'
A long, long way from home
a long way from
a long way from
sometimes I feel like I'm
a long, long way from
Sometimes I feel like a motherless chil'
Sometimes I feel like I'm a
a long way from home
sometimes I feel like a motherless chil'

Sometimes I feel like I'm almost gone
sometimes I feel
sometimes I feel like
sometimes I feel like I'm almost gone
Tellin' you sometimes I feel like I'm almost gone
sometimes I feel
sometimes I feel like
sometimes I feel like I'm almost gone
Well, sometimes I feel like I'm almost gone
sometimes I feel
sometimes I feel like
sometimes I feel like I'm almost gone

And I'm a long, long way from home
a long way
a long way
sometimes I feel like I'm

Sometimes I feel like I'm almost gone
a long, long way from
Sometimes I feel like I'm a
a long way from home
Sometimes I feel like a motherless chil'

Oh true believer, true believer, true believer,
I'm a long way from home
True believer, true believer, true believer
A long way from home
Oh true believer, true believer,
I'm a long way from home
I'm a long, long way
True believer, true believer, true believer
A long way from home

Sometimes I feel like I'm almost gone
sometimes I feel
sometimes I feel like
sometimes I feel like I'm almost gone
Tellin' you sometimes I feel like I'm almost gone
sometimes I feel
sometimes I feel like
sometimes I feel like I'm almost gone
Well, sometimes I feel like I'm almost gone
sometimes I feel
sometimes I feel like
sometimes I feel like I'm almost gone
And I'm a long, long way from home
a long way
a long way
sometimes I feel like I'm
Sometimes I feel like I'm almost gone
a long, long way from
Sometimes I feel like I'm a
a long way from home
But I can hear my Mother callin' me
sometimes I feel like a motherless chil'

She's callin' me. I can hear my Mother's voice. I can
hear my Mother's voice and she's callin' me and I...
I can hear her calling me,
I can hear her calling me,
hear her calling me,
A long way from home
I can hear my Mother. She's callin' me
Oh, won't you come on home chil', 'cross the waters,
I can hear her calling me,
I can hear her calling me,
hear her calling me,
But I'm a long, a long way from home
A long way from home

Well, sometimes
Sometimes I feel like a - sometimes I feel just like I'm a
motherless chil', motherless chil'
sometimes I feel
sometimes I feel like
sometimes I feel like a motherless chil'
Tellin' you sometimes I feel like a motherless chil'.
Lord knows.
Lord knows I'm a motherless chil' Hey Hey Hey Hey
Oh Oh
sometimes I feel

sometimes I feel like
sometimes I feel like a motherless chil'
Sometimes I feel like a motherless chil'
sometimes I feel
sometimes I feel like
sometimes I feel like a motherless chil'
**Hey but you know I'm a long way from home, but I
can hear my mother's voice callin' me back, chil'**
a long way from

a long way from
sometimes I feel like I'm
a long, long way from
**Come on home. Come on home. I miss you chil' but
I'm a long way from home**
Sometimes I feel like I'm a
a long way from home
Sometimes I feel like a motherless chil'.
Sometimes I feel like a motherless chil'.

COMPOSER'S NOTES

STAY

"Stay" is a Nouveau Doo-Wop song. Not as rigid in form but it definitely has a slow-dance-under-the-light-bulb feel in terms of style. Finger snaps help a lot.

I'm very much in touch with the spiritual aspect of love and loving. Many times, the illusion and glamour of what we think is love is actually a delusion. We are attracted to form, to packaging, to passion and pleasure. These things can enhance feelings of attractiveness, but they are not what love is. Love exists solely for love's sake – pure, unattached and open, wanting only the best in all situations. It uplifts. Love is an expanding, empowering energy. It takes great courage to love with one life, one breath, one spirit, one heart.

"Stay" can be sung as a spiritual song as well. Take out the word baby whenever it appears and think of the Lord and you'll know where this song originated. Make sure the bass is solid and strong. Keep the trio crisp, but very, very sweet. Let the lead establish the melody in verse one. And then stretch out on verse two. Croon it to your sweetest heart or your beloved Lord. Pure love knows no bounds!

PRAYER TO THE ONE

One morning, after working all night on another arrangement, this song came very spontaneously. I simply began singing the words and melody, and I found that I was able to remember them enough to write them down as "Prayer to the One."

The song has an unusual rhythm. You have to hear the inhalation (on the first beat) before singing each line. Although there is limited rhythmic accompaniment on the recording (*Sacred Ground*), I originally heard other instruments and sounds, particularly during the vocal improvisation. The feeling is definitely Brazilian, and the lead vocal should feel free to explore those rhythms with the other members of the ensemble. In a small group (5-10 singers), make sure the improvisation is clean and complementary. Don't set it too concretely. That kills the joy of it. Find, perhaps, one or two lines that can be fairly stable. The obligato line (sung by Aisha Kahlil on the recording) rides over the group, and the lead is free to improvise from the top line all the way down to the bass line, or lower if possible, and back up again. Listening is very important in the improvisation sections. These sections are not a competition but a cooperative process of creation.

The song begins with one voice and as each voice enters, there should be a seamless blend, one voice, one breath, no separation.

Meister Ekert, a philosopher, said: "The eye with which I see God is the same eye with which God sees me..."

This song was written based on the teachings of many East Indian spiritual masters who tell us there is no difference between the one who loves and the one who is loved. We look outside of ourselves for satisfaction and fulfillment, but we only need to tap the source of light and joy that exists within as our very own self. God is everywhere in everything and is as close as our very breath.

This song was dedicated to my own dear meditation teacher.

GOIN' TO SEE MY BABY

I'm at 16th and P Streets in Northwest Washington, D.C., on my way to meet my boyfriend. He and I write poetry and lyrics all the time, and I'm on my way to meet him, yes I am. The bus is slow. I am anxious. I don't care how I get there. I know I've gotta make this journey to where he is. I'm coming, baby, I'm on my way. We were so connected, spiritually, psychically. I knew he was waiting for and thinking about me with the same intensity... Voila! A song! Enjoy it!

MOTHERLESS CHIL'

"Motherless Chil'" is a song I've known since I was very small. Not having been raised by my own mother, it always had a special message for me, especially when I found myself longing to hear from or see her.

The song is a Spiritual, but I think of it as a sorrow song (see the writings of W.E.B. DuBois). My friend Fontella Boone visited Senegal and shared with me her experience of visiting the Ile de Gorée. Gorée is the place where African men, women and children were held before boarding the slave ships that would take them across the Atlantic. Can you imagine it? Visualize it? Put yourself there in the dark, small room, crowded and hot, with no idea of the wretchedness of what was to come. I cry when I think of it, when I imagine my son missing or stolen from me. It puts me in touch with the plight and also the strength of my own ancestors.

'Mother' in verse five is not only Mother in the literal, biological sense, but in the sense of Africa being Mother to humanity. Not just to Africans but to all humanity.

There is a sense of inner contemplation in the beginning. There is quiet and sadness that builds as the song progresses and comes full circle to the same feeling at the end. The chorus is the driving force behind the song, supports its power, drives the energy to its peak, provides a bed of sound upon which the soloist can explore their feelings and experience the lyrics. The background can actually exist without the lead and vice-versa, but together they weave a beautiful and powerful tapestry of sound, emotion and history.

This arrangement of "Motherless Chil'" should have a lead that understands the lyrics not just intellectually but on a true emotional level. This will give the song a contemporary feel and a sense of immediacy, honesty and truth.

Stay

Words and Music by
Carol Maillard

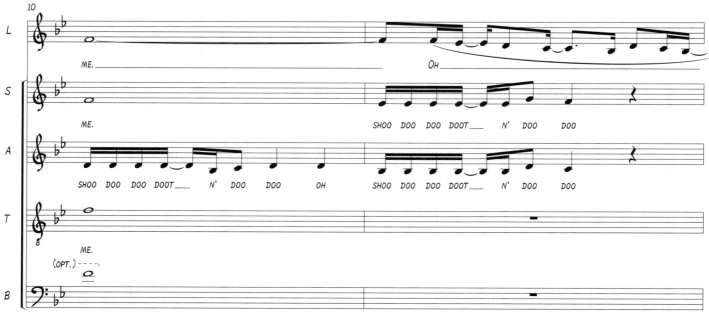

2. *One light, one breath, one spirit, one heart*
One love lives between us
When you drink, my thirst is satisfied,
And when I tire, I know that
You'll be there to give me rest
Just to live my life with you
Would be so sweet, so divine
Like the sounds of the wind
Whistlin' through the trees
Ancestor rhythms, the sound of two hearts
Dancing love's dance together
Time is movin' on, but I'm asking you to
Stay.

Prayer To The One

Words and Music by Carol Maillard

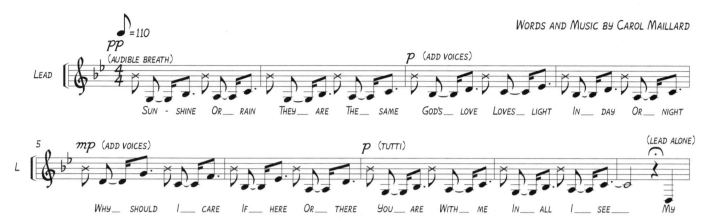

* THESE LINES ARE TRANSCRIBED VERBATIM FROM THE PERFORMANCE ON
SWEET HONEY'S RECORDING "SACRED GROUND;" THEY ARE INTENDED AS GUIDES,
AND ARE NOT MEANT TO BE STRICTLY ADHERED TO AS WRITTEN. SPECIFIC NOTES,
RHYTHMS, AND SYLLABLES ARE UP TO THE PERFORMERS.

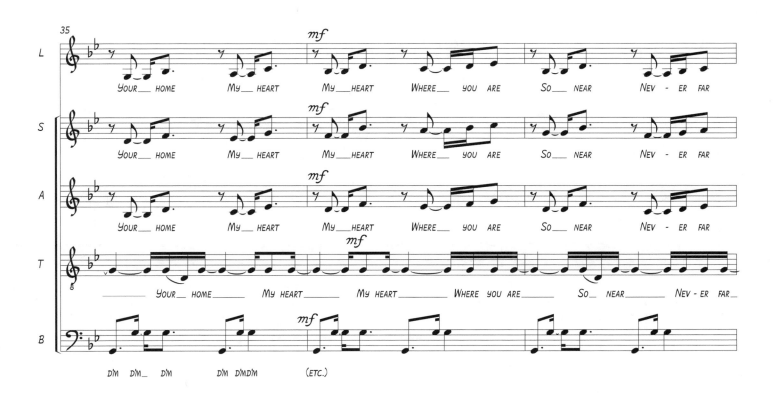

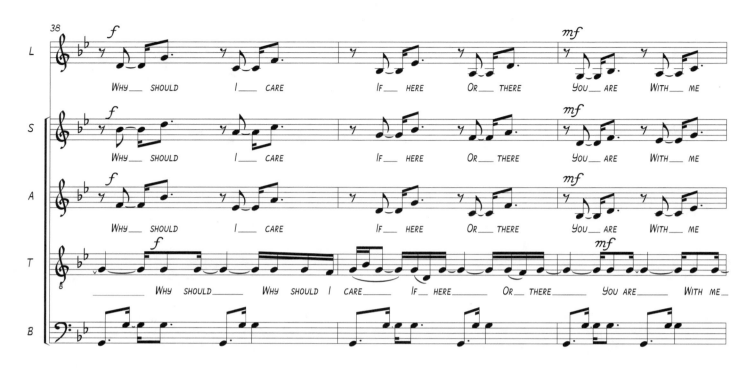

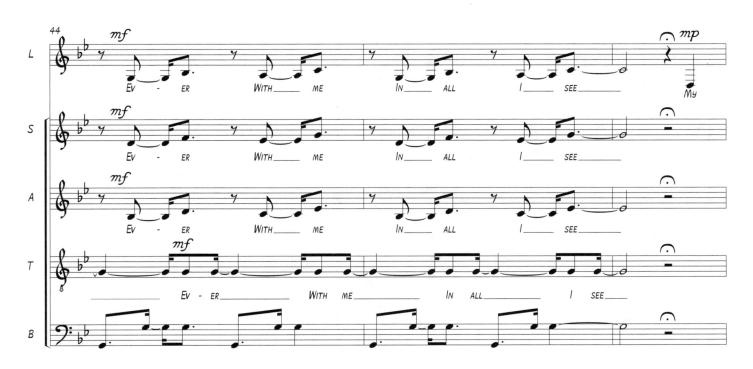

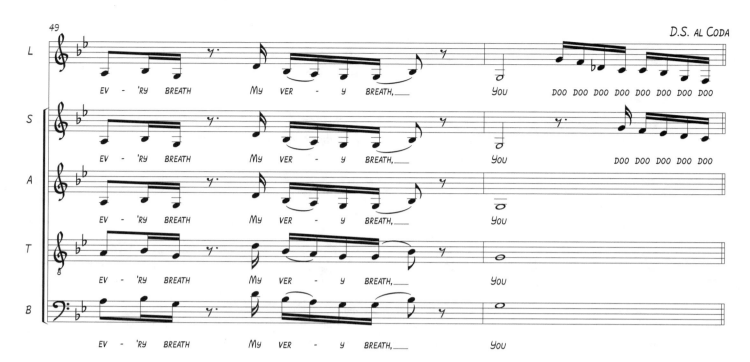

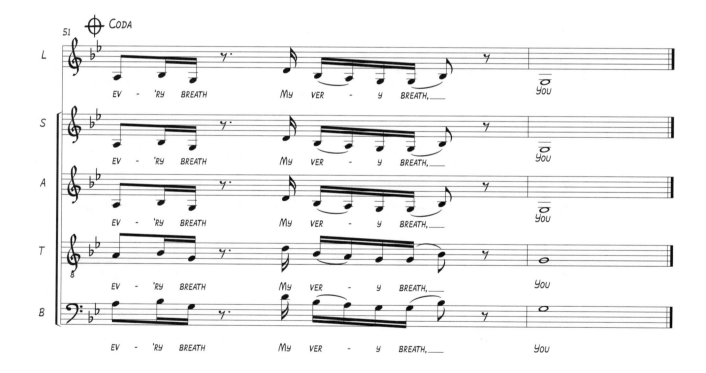

Goin' To See My Baby

Words and Music by Carol Maillard

Motherless Chil'

TRADITIONAL SPIRITUAL
ARRANGED BY CAROL MAILLARD

BERNICE JOHNSON REAGON
ELLA'S SONG · SOMETIME
I REMEMBER, I BELIEVE · NO MORE AUCTION BLOCK (TRAD./ARR.)

BERNICE JOHNSON REAGON, scholar, composer, singer and activist, is Distinguished Professor of History at American University and Curator Emeritus at the Smithsonian Institution, National Museum of American History. During the Civil Rights Movement, Reagon was a member of the original SNCC (Student Non-Violent Coordinating Committee) Freedom Singers, and in 1965 she was a founding member of the Harambee Singers, an a cappella ensemble of Black women based in Atlanta, Georgia. Dr. Reagon continues to perform with Sweet Honey In The Rock, the world-renowned a cappella ensemble she founded in 1973.

Reagon was featured in the 1992 Emmy-nominated *The Songs are Free: Bernice Johnson Reagon with Bill Moyers*, a 60-minute production of Public Affairs Television. She has served as music consultant, composer and/or performer for several film and video projects, including *Beloved*, directed by Jonathan Demme; the award-winning *Eyes On The Prize*, produced by Blackside Productions the Emmy-winning *We Shall Overcome*, produced by Ginger Productions for PBS; *Roots of Resistance: A Story of the Underground Railroad* and *Frederick Douglass: The Lion Who Wrote History*, both produced by Orlando Bagwell, Roja Productions for PBS. In 1989, she was awarded a MacArthur Fellowship for her work as an artist and scholar of African-American culture. Reagon received a Presidential Medal in 1995, the Charles E. Frankel Prize for outstanding contribution to public understanding of the humanities. In 1996, Reagon received an Isadora Duncan award for her creation of the score to *Rock*, a ballet directed by Alonzo King for LINES Contemporary Ballet Company.

Reagon served as principal scholar, conceptual producer and host of the path-breaking Smithsonian Institution and National Public Radio series *Wade In The Water: African-American Sacred Music Traditions*, which began to air in January 1994. The series received the prestigious 1994 Peabody Award for Significance and Meritorious Achievement in Broadcasting. Reagon also compiled and composed the score for *Africans in America*, the 1998 PBS film series on American Slavery produced by WGBH in Boston.

Dr. Reagon's publications include: We Who Believe In Freedom: Sweet Honey In The Rock – 20 Years and Still On The Journey (Anchor Books, 1993); We'll Understand It Better By and By: Pioneering African-American Gospel Composers (Smithsonian Press, 1992); *Voices of the Civil Rights Movement: Black American Freedom Songs 1960-1965*, a newly re-released two-CD collection with accom-panying booklet and *Wade In The Water*, a four-CD anthology of 19th and 20th century African-American sacred music (both on Smithsonian Folkways Recordings, 1997); and Compositions One: The Original Compositions and Arrangements of Bernice Johnson Reagon (1986).

Among Reagon's solo recordings are *Give Your Hands to Struggle*, (1975, re-released on Smithsonian Folkways Recordings, 1997) and *River of Life* (Flying Fish, 1986). In addition to her work as singer and composer on all of Sweet Honey In The Rock's recordings, Dr. Reagon has served as producer on several of the group's more than 14 recordings.

Dr. Reagon currently resides in Washington, D.C.

ELLA'S SONG
LYRICS AND MUSIC BY BERNICE JOHNSON REAGON

CHORUS
We who believe in freedom
cannot rest
We who believe in freedom
cannot rest until it comes.

VERSES

Until the killing of Black men,
Black mothers' sons
Is as important as the killing of White men,
White mothers' sons.

That which touches me most
is that I had a chance to work with people
Passing on to others
that which was passed on to me.

To me young people come first,
they have the courage where we failed
And if I can but shed some light
as they carry us through the gale.

The older I get, the better I know that
the secret of my going on
Is when the reins are in the hands of the young
who dare to run against the storm.

Not needing to clutch for power,
not needing the light just to shine on me,
I need to be one in the number
as we stand against tyranny.

Struggling myself don't mean a whole lot,
I've come to realize
that teaching others to stand up and fight is
the only way my struggle survives.

I'm a woman who speaks in a voice
and I must be heard
At times I can be quite difficult,
I'll bow to no man's word.

SOMETIME

LYRICS AND MUSIC BY BERNICE JOHNSON REAGON

Sometime day breaks in my life
Sometime the sun shines in my life
Sometime things work right in my life
You are my sometime
You are my sometime
You are my sometime

When shackles fall from my heart
When the rock seems to roll from my way
When I find myself open to love
You are my when
You are my when
You are my when

For the ending of being alone
for the believing in the smiles and warmth I feel
For our leavings to come back again
You are my for
You are my for
You are my for

Sometime don't come every day
When seems to never get here at all
For is the future that I could never face
and you bring them all to me
You are my sometime
You are my when
You are my forever

I REMEMBER, I BELIEVE

LYRICS AND MUSIC BY BERNICE JOHNSON REAGON

I don' know how my mother walked her trouble down
I don' know how my father stood his ground
I don' know how my people survived slavery
I do remember, that's why I believe.

I don' know why the rivers overflow their banks
I don' know why the snow falls and covers the ground
I don' know why the hurricane sweeps through the land
every now and then
Standing in a rainstorm, I believe.

I don' know why the angels woke me up this morning soon
I don' know why the blood still runs through my veins
I don' know how I rate to run another day
I am here still running, I believe.

My God calls to me in the morning dew
The power of the universe knows my name
Gave me a song to sing and sent me on my way
I raise my voice for justice, I believe.

NO MORE AUCTION BLOCK

TRAD. SPIRITUAL / ARR.
BY BERNICE JOHNSON REAGON

CHORUS
No more auction block for me.
No more, no more
No more auction block for me.
Many thousands gone.

VERSES
And oh, the one thing that we did wrong,
No more, no more
Stayed in the wilderness a day too long.
No more, no more.

And oh, the one thing that we did right
Oh yes, oh yes my Lord
Was the day that we began to fight!
Oh yes, oh yes my Lord.

COMPOSER'S NOTES

ELLA'S SONG

In 1980, I received a call from Joanne Grant, who was making the film *Fundi* about Ella Josephine Baker, a woman who had for more than 50 years worked as an organizing leader against racism and injustice in the United States. Grant wanted to send me a rough cut of the film and asked me to score it. Soon it arrived and I was looking at her at different stages of her work during the Civil Rights Movement, speaking about freedom, speaking about the importance of organizing, telling all who would hear that Black people had a right to come together and decide what we should do about the issues we faced daily.

I had met Ella Baker during my early days in the Civil Rights Movement. She had a big impact on my life, as she did for most of those of the Student Non-Violent Coordinating Committee. She was a leader who taught us that leading often meant not being the voice of the people.

Sometimes leading meant making it possible for others to come forth. Sometimes leading meant listening to others, especially young people. Ella Baker believed young people should be given the space to define the times they lived in and find ways to get involved in shaping the world in which they found themselves, that older people needed to support and help provide this kind of space and opportunity for young people and that older people could often be taught and sometimes pulled along by the young among us.

The lyrics for "Ella's Song" are based on the lessons I received from the teachings of Ella Baker, and it formed the theme of the film. The refrain for "Ella's Song" was based on a speech in which she talked about the killing of Civil Rights workers in Mississippi in 1964. James Chaney, Andrew Goodman and Michael Schwerner were killed while investigating the burning of a church whose members had allowed it to be used for

a voter registration meeting. When they went missing, a cry went up from the Movement and from people throughout the USA to find them. During the search, they began to drag the rivers of Mississippi, and though they did not turn up the bodies of these three young men, they did turn up bodies of other Black men who had been killed that no one had ever looked for. James Chaney was Black and a native of Mississippi. Andrew Schwerner and Michael Goodman were White and Jewish from New York. During the search, Rita Schwerner, the wife of Andrew, said that had the Civil Rights team been all Black, we probably would have never been able to force such a massive search. The bodies were found in a crude earthen dam. The families of Schwerner and Goodman asked that their sons be buried with James Chaney. It did not happen, because at that time cemeteries in Mississippi were segregated. Although these men were massacred together, it was against the law for them to be buried together.

Ella Baker made this statement, and I knew I had the refrain for the song: "Until the killing of Black men, Black mothers' sons, is as important as the killing of White men, White mothers' sons, we who believe in freedom cannot rest, until this happens."

SOMETIME

I wrote "Sometime" on the occasion of the marriage of my friends James Morris and Cynthia Hightower. As I talked to them separately about what this step meant to them, they both talked not so much euphorically but about how being together meant no longer traveling alone. Because they were together now, sometimes life was easier, the sun came up brighter, sometimes; sometimes I find myself opening up like a new flower, and these sometimes are enough for me to want my tomorrows to be with you. This is a commitment song – beyond falling in love – of that rare and special time when two people choose to join and move through their lives as bonded partners. It is truly something to celebrate.

I REMEMBER, I BELIEVE

One Sunday morning, Dr. A. Knighton Stanley of the People's Congregational Church in Washington, D.C. preached a sermon based on the Hebraic tradition of remembering as the basis of faith. I was struck because he seemed to be saying that practicing history could be the basis of believing. He told the story of Elie Wiesel who said that although one may not have been in the concentration camps, one could live as if that was part of your personal history. As I sat there, the thought came to me that I had not actually been on one of those ships that brought my people in chains across the Atlantic during that horrific Middle Passage, but I did try to live my life as if that was part of my personal makeup. The sermon also gave me a new way of looking at my existence today. It invited me to understand my life as evidence of the success of my ancestors. Somehow with all they faced, day to day, they made enough of the right choices so that I am here today, evidence of the success of their lives and struggles. It made me responsible as a contemporary representative of the great human struggle against evil. It made me believe that if, day by day, my people who came before me met as best they could the challenges they faced so that I am here today, then I could in my life, day by day, have faith that I could handle what life and society put on my plate. It also made me believe that I could respond in such a way that there might be a chance for my children's children's children to move in their lives as among other things — evidence of the success of my efforts.

I have tried to phonetically reconstruct the sounds that open this song and that I also sing in performance after the third and last text cycles and at the end after the last cycle. All of the lines are straight out of the quartet tradition except the top part. This line works best as a line that is explicated with a lot of air, sort of a whisper but a very intense one. If you do not have a singer who understands this upon listening to me perform it on the Sweet Honey In The Rock recording *Sacred Ground*, then perform it as a shadow line, very softly lacing the rest of the chord.

NO MORE AUCTION BLOCK

I set this 19th century declarative freedom song cry for Sweet Honey In The Rock in 1975, when the members were Carol Lynn Maillard, Patricia Johnson, Tia Juana Starks, Evelyn Maria Harris and me. The song itself was important to me. I was a young adult when I learned it. It was one of the first songs I heard created by my people that was so frontal, no code, no covering, just right out there for all to know what we felt about slavery and about that evil thing that twisted our lives and threatened at any time to rip apart any fragile bonding we had been able to snatch with our partners, our children, our parents, our friends.

It was important for me as a child of the 20th century to stand in the sound of this song, to give voice to this song, and to know my people were clear and articulate about the evils of American slavery. As we move toward the end of the century, this concern might seem unusual. However, as children growing up in the South, we went through an educational system that presented a strange picture of African-Americans and the slave system. In my 11th grade history textbook, a sentence jumped out at me, 'almost' knocking me down. It said we were better off as slaves in America than as free people in Africa, because in Africa we ate each other. I say 'almost' because my teacher, Ms. Olive Rogers, said in a soft voice (clear enough for all of us to hear) "Well, I don't know about that!"

It may not sound like much, but that statement, which questioned Georgia's approved history textbook, planted in me a small seed of resistance that lay dormant until it was nurtured by this song, "No More Auction Block For Me."

In this arrangement, I apply a principle that I have long held, that every singer's full range gives her or him access to low, middle and high lines based on the key. There may be a place in your voice where you feel most comfortable, where you can operate with optimal control, power and flexibility; however, I believe in a decent choral experience, a singer should have the opportunity to exercise her/his full range.

In "Auction Block," each verse was set so that the chorus, in sound range, follows the song leader. For example, in the third cycle of the song (first verse), the lead is in the soprano voice and the chorus shifts up into a high harmony trio, then moves to the middle range for the next verse and finally down to a low harmony palette for the coda cycle of the composition. The score is presented so that you can have everyone shifting to try out the different palettes, or assign choruses by traditional vocal sections, which they then hold throughout the piece.

All choruses are led by a solo voice. The first chorus is set in congregational style, opened by a solo voice as song leader. Once that voice begins the song, everyone joins in and it is sung together in harmony. The second chorus, a second statement of the central theme, has the solo voice in a lead position throughout. In this arrangement, I have tried to restore my original intent of having the other voices in the chorus fall in a kind of scattered effect after the lead voice. If you listen to this song on the *Sacred Ground* recording, you will find this verse is set with the chorus in a simple echo pattern with the lead.

The third verse features the high trio responding to a lead by a soprano. This is followed by a verse led by a contralto. The response operates in its own time, directed by its own lead or melody line; the lead moving on top – sometimes in front, sometimes extending beyond the choral patterns. The last chorus is led by a low voice, and the choral response shifts down and answers in the traditional call and response pattern.

Ella's Song

Bernice Johnson Reagon

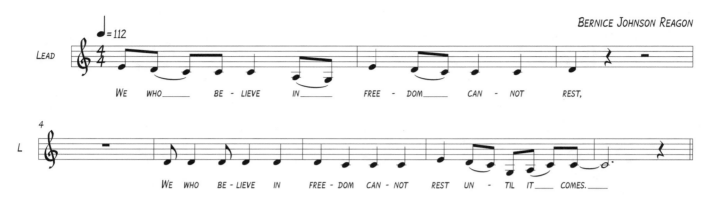

We who____ be - lieve in____ free - dom____ can - not rest,

We who be - lieve in free - dom can - not rest un - til it____ comes.____

Refrain:

L: We who____ be - lieve in____ free - dom____ can - not rest,____

Soprano: We who____ be - lieve in free - dom____ can - not rest,

Alto: We who____ be - lieve in free - dom____ can - not rest,

Tenor: We who be - lieve in free - dom can - not rest,

Bass: We who be - lieve____ in____ free - dom can - not____ rest,

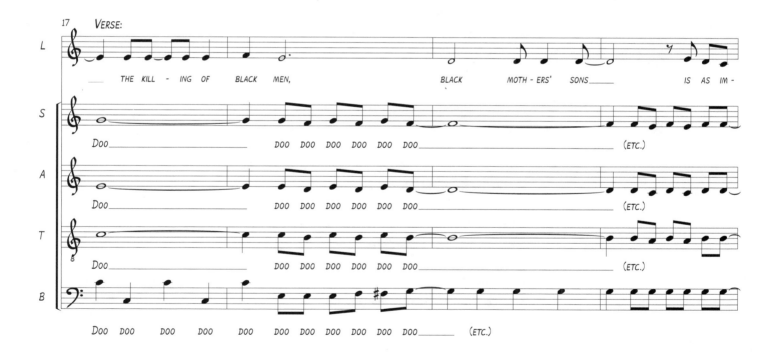

POR - TANT AS THE KILL - ING OF WHITE____ MEN,_____ WHITE____ MOTH - ERS' SONS.____

2. *That which touches me most is that I had a chance to work with people*
   Passing on to others that which was passed on to me.

3. *To me young people come first, they have the courage where we failed*
   And If I can but shed some light as they carry us through the Gale.

4. *The older I get, the better I know that the secret of my going on*
   Is when the reins are in the hands of the young who dare to run against the storm.

5. *Not needing to clutch for power, not needing the light just to shine on me,*
   I need to be one in the number as we stand against tyranny.

6. *Struggling myself don't mean a whole lot, I've come to realize*
   That teaching others to stand up and fight is the only way our struggle survives.

7. *I'm a woman who speaks in a voice, and I must be heard;*
   at times I can be quite difficult, I'll bow to no man's word.

Sometime

Words and Music by
Bernice Johnson Reagon

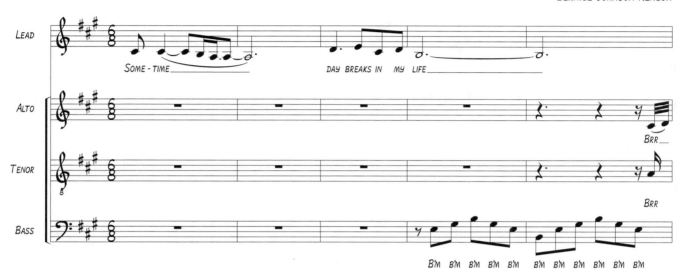

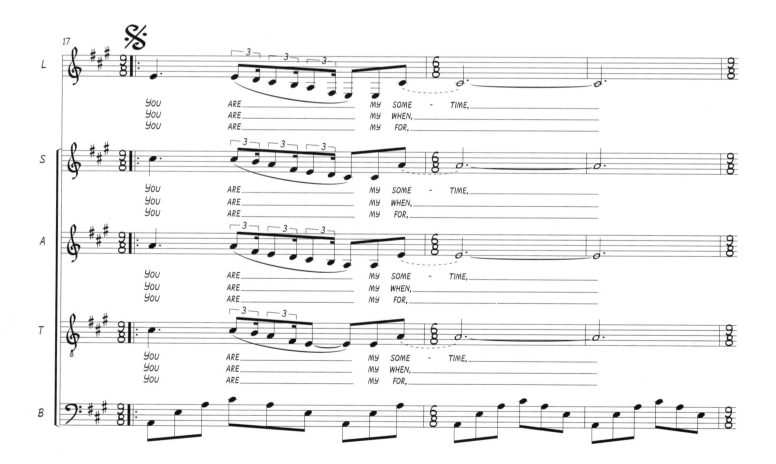

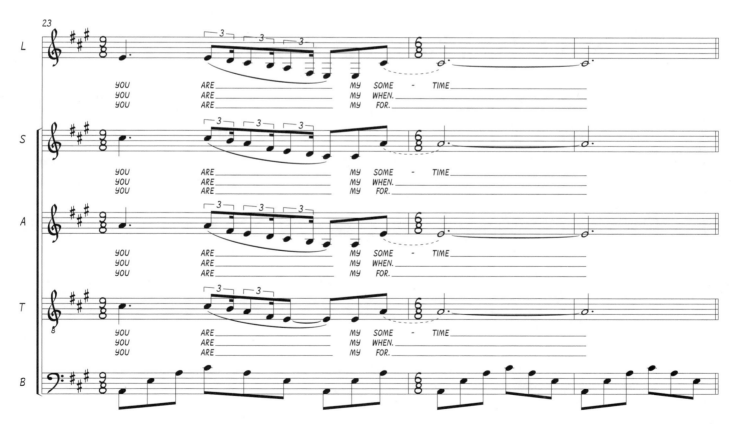

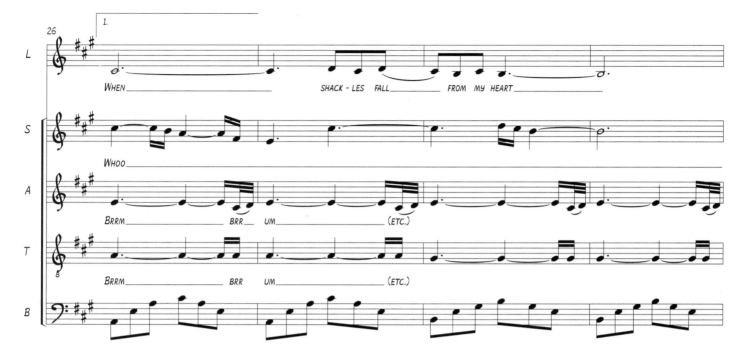

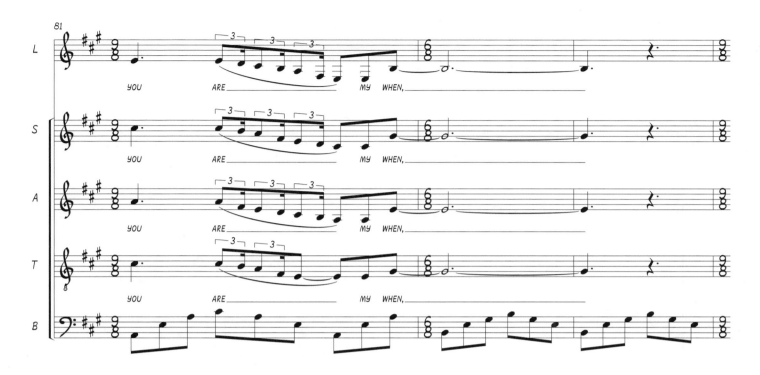

I Remember, I Believe

NOTE: THE SOPRANO (TOP) LINE IS A BREATHY BUT INTENSE "AIR" LINE THAT LACES AND ANSWERS THE MAIN BODY OF THE SONG. SOME OF ITS TEXT ARE SOUNDS. (LIKE SOFT 'H', 'D', AND 'B'). LYRICS ARE DELIVERED WITH A SOFT PERCUSSIVE QUALITY.

WORDS AND MUSIC BY
BERNICE JOHNSON REAGON

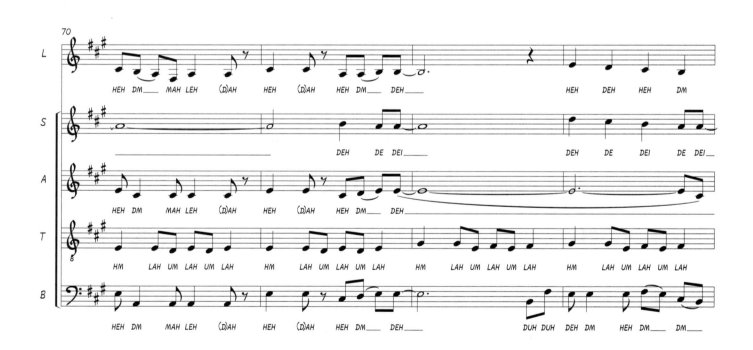

2. I DON' KNOW WHY THE RIVERS OVERFLOW THEIR BANKS

   I DON' KNOW WHY THE SNOW FALLS AND COVERS THE GROUND

   I DON' KNOW WHY THE HURRICANE SWEEPS THROUGH THE LAND EVERY NOW AND THEN

   STANDING IN THE RAINSTORM, I BELIEVE.

3. I DON' KNOW WHY THE ANGELS WOKE ME UP THIS MORNING SOON

   I DON' KNOW WHY THE BLOOD STILL RUNS THROUGH MY VEINS

   I DON' KNOW HOW I RATE TO RUN ANOTHER DAY

   I AM HERE STILL RUNNIN', I BELIEVE.

No More Auction Block

NOTE: EACH VERSE IS LED BY A DIFFERENT LEAD SINGER. ON REPEAT OF FIRST CHORUS,
LEAD STAYS JUST IN FRONT OF THE CHORUS IN A CALL AND RESPONSE PATTERN.

ARRANGED BY BERNICE JOHNSON REAGON

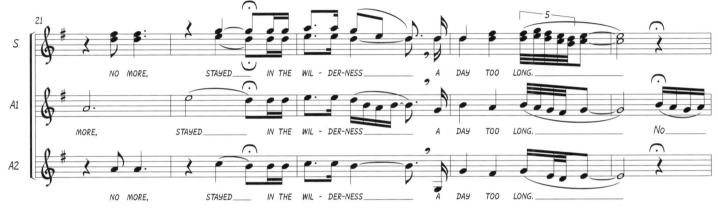

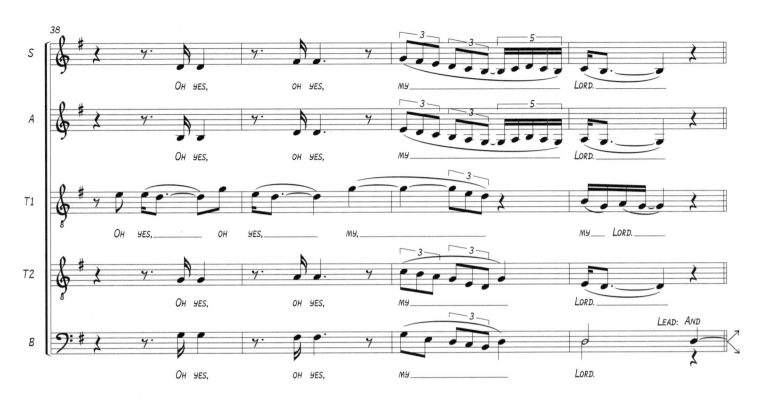

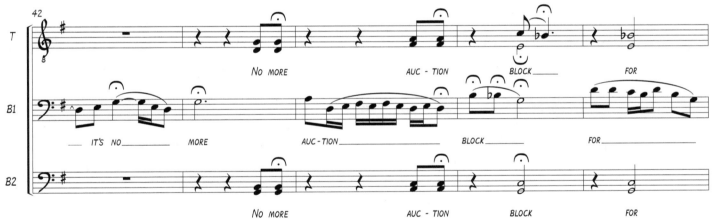

DISCOGRAPHY OF THE SONGS

(as recorded by Sweet Honey In The Rock)

ALUNDE
All for Freedom (Music For Little People 1989)

BREATHS
Good News (Flying Fish 1981)
Breaths (Flying Fish 1988)
Selections (Rounder 1997)

CUM BA YAH
All for Freedom (Music For Little People 1989)

DENKO
Live at Carnegie Hall (Flying Fish 1988)
Selections (Rounder 1997)

DREAM SONGS OF LOVE
Live at Carnegie Hall (Flying Fish 1988)

ELLA'S SONG
We All...Everyone Of Us (Flying Fish 1983)
Selections (Rounder 1997)

FULANI CHANT
In This Land (EarthBeat! 1992)

GOIN' TO SEE MY BABY
Sweet Honey In The Rock (Flying Fish 1976)

INNER VOICES
Sacred Ground (EarthBeat! 1996)

I REMEMBER, I BELIEVE
Sacred Ground (EarthBeat! 1996)

MOTHERLESS CHIL'
...TWENTY-FIVE... (Rykodisc 1998)

NO MORE AUCTION BLOCK
Sacred Ground (EarthBeat! 1996)

PRAYER TO THE ONE
Sacred Ground (EarthBeat! 1996)

RUN
...TWENTY-FIVE... (Rykodisc 1998)

SOMETIME
Good News (Flying Fish 1981)
Breaths (Flying Fish 1988)
Selections (Rounder 1997)
...TWENTY-FIVE... (Rykodisc 1998)

STAY
Still On The Journey (EarthBeat! 1993)

WE ARE...
Sacred Ground (EarthBeat! 1996)

WODAABE NIGHTS
Still On The Journey (EarthBeat! 1993)

WOULD YOU HARBOR ME?
Sacred Ground (EarthBeat! 1996)

YOUNG AND POSITIVE
I Got Shoes (Music For Little People 1994)

PHOTO BY DWIGHT CARTER

SWEET HONEY IN THE ROCK
- DISCOGRAPHY

SWEET HONEY IN THE ROCK
(FLYING FISH 1976)
Sweet Honey In The Rock
The Sun Will Never Go Down
Dream Variations
Let Us All Come Together
Joanne Little
Jesus Is My Only Friend
Are There Any Rights I'm Entitled To
Going to See My Baby
You Make My Day Pretty
Hey Mann
Doing Things Together
Traveling Shoes
Sweet Honey In the Rock-II

B'LIEVE I'LL RUN ON... (REDWOOD 1978)
Seven Principles
A Woman
Fannie Lou Hamer
My Way
They Are Falling All Around Me
B'lieve I'll Run On
All Praise Is Due to Love
Sitting on Top of the World
Every Woman

GOOD NEWS (FLYING FISH 1981)
Breaths
Echo
Chile Your Waters Run Red Through Soweto
Oh Death
Biko
If You Had Lived
Oughta Be a Woman
On Children
Time On My Hands
Alla That's All Right, But
Sometime

WE ALL...EVERYONE OF US
(FLYING FISH 1983)
Study War No More
What a Friend We Have in Jesus
Sweet Bird of Youth
How Long?
More than a Paycheck
Azanian Freedom Song
Listen to the Rhythm
Testimony
Oh Lord, Hold My Hand
Battle For My Life
Ella's Song
I'm Gon' Stand
We All...Everyone of Us

THE OTHER SIDE (FLYING FISH 1985)
Mandiacapella
Step by Step
Deportees
Moving On
Stranger Blues
Venceremos
The Other Side
No Images
Gift of Love
Mae Frances
Ol' Landmark
Tomorrow

BREATHS (CD ONLY)
(FLYING FISH 1988)
includes songs from:
GOOD NEWS and
WE ALL...EVERYONE OF US

FEEL SOMETHING DRAWING ME ON
(FLYING FISH 1985)
We'll Understand It Better, By And By
Father I Stretch My Hands to Thee
Hush Lil' Baby
I've Got to Know
When I Die Tomorrow
Meyango
Waters of Babylon (Rivers of Babylon)
Feel Something Drawing Me On
Try Jesus
Leaning and Depending On The Lord
In the Upper Room

LIVE AT CARNEGIE HALL
(FLYING FISH 1988)
Beatitudes
Run, Run, Mourner Run
Wade in the Water
Drinking of the Wine
Where Are The Keys to the Kingdom
Dream Songs of Love
Letter to Dr. Martin Luther King
Emergency
Our Side Won
Ode to the International Debt
Are My Hands Clean?
Denko
Your Worries Ain't Like Mine
My Lament
Song of the Exiled
Peace

ALL FOR FREEDOM
(MUSIC FOR LITTLE PEOPLE 1989)
So Glad I'm Here
Cum Ba Yah
Down in the Valley Two by Two
The Little Shekere
The Little Red Caboose
All For Freedom
Juba
Everybody Ought to Know
Calypso Freedom
Amen
Ise Oluwa
Meeting at the Building
Johanna and Rhody
Make New Friends
Horse and Buggy
Silvie
Alunde and the Story of Ono